500 FACTS
Planet
Earth

500 FACTS
Planet
Earth

First published in 2009 by Miles Kelly Publishing Ltd
Bardfield Centre, Great Bardfield, Essex, CM7 4SL

Copyright © Miles Kelly Publishing Ltd 2009

The sections in this book are also available as individual titles

2 4 6 8 10 9 7 5 3 1

Editorial Director Belinda Gallagher
Art Director Jo Brewer
Editions Manager Bethan Ellish
Editors Carly Blake, Rosie McGuire
Cover Designer Simon Lee
Designers John Christopher (White Design),
Simon Lee, Sophie Pelham, Elaine Wilkinson
Indexer Eleanor Holme
Production Manager Elizabeth Brunwin
Reprographics Stephan Davis, Jennifer Hunt, Ian Paulyn
Contributors Camilla de la Bedoyere, Clive Carpenter, Anna Claybourne,
Clare Oliver, Steve Parker, Peter Riley, Barbara Taylor

ISBN 978-1-84810-201-9

Printed in China

British Library Cataloguing-in-Publication Data
A catalogue record for this book is available from the British Library

Made with paper from a sustainable forest

www.mileskelly.net
info@mileskelly.net

www.factsforprojects.com
The one-stop homework helper —
pictures, facts, videos, projects and more

Contents

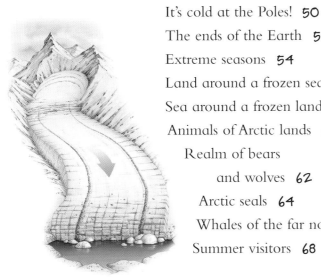

OCEANS 92–133

RAINFORESTS 134–175

SAVING THE EARTH 176–217

ACKNOWLEDGEMENTS 224

The speedy space ball

1 The Earth is a huge ball of rock moving through space at nearly 3000 metres per second. It weighs 6000 million, million, million tonnes. Up to two-thirds of the Earth's rocky surface is covered by water – this makes the seas and oceans. Rock that is not covered by water makes the land. Surrounding the Earth is a layer of gases called the atmosphere (air). This reaches about 700 kilometres from the Earth's surface – then space begins.

▶ Mercury, the planet nearest to the Sun, is small and hot. Venus and Earth are rocky and cooler.

Venus

Mercury

Sun

Where did Earth come from?

2 **The Earth came from a cloud in space.**
Scientists think the Earth formed from a huge cloud of gas and dust around 4500 million years ago. A star near the cloud exploded, making the cloud spin. As the cloud spun around, gases gathered at its centre and formed the Sun. Dust whizzed around the Sun and stuck together to form lumps of rock. In time the rocks crashed into each other to make the planets. The Earth is one of these planets.

5. The Earth was made up of one large piece of land, now split into seven chunks known as continents

1. Cloud starts to spin

▶ Clouds of gas and dust are made by the remains of old stars that have exploded or simply stopped shining. It is here that new stars and their planets form.

4. Volcanoes erupt, releasing gases, helping to form the first atmosphere

3. The Earth begins to cool and a hard shell forms

3 **At first the Earth was very hot.** As the rocks crashed together they warmed each other up. Later, as the Earth formed, the rocks inside it melted. The new Earth was a ball of liquid rock with a thin, solid shell.

2. Dust gathers into lumps of rock which form a small planet

4 Huge numbers of large rocks called meteorites crashed into the Earth. They made round hollows on the surface. These hollows are called craters. The Moon was hit with rocks at the same time. Look at the Moon with binoculars – you can see the craters that were made long ago.

▶ The Moon was also hit by rocks in space, and these made huge craters, and mountain ranges up to 5000 metres high.

▼ Erupting volcanoes and fierce storms helped form the atmosphere and oceans. These provided energy that was needed for life on Earth to begin.

5 The oceans and seas formed as the Earth cooled down. Volcanoes erupted, letting out steam, gases and rocks from inside the Earth. As the Earth cooled, the steam changed to water droplets and made clouds. As the Earth cooled further, rain fell from the clouds. It rained for millions of years to make the seas and oceans.

I DON'T BELIEVE IT!

Millions of rocks crash into Earth as it speeds through space. Some larger ones may reach the ground as meteorites.

In a spin

6 **The Earth is like a huge spinning top.** It continues to spin because it was formed from a spinning cloud of gas and dust. It does not spin straight up like a top but leans a little to one side. The Earth takes 24 hours to spin around once. We call this period of time a day.

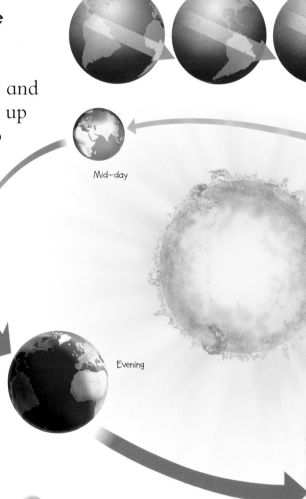

Mid-day

Evening

7 **The Earth's spinning makes day and night.** Each part of the Earth spins towards the Sun, and then away from it every day. When a part of the Earth is facing the Sun it is day-time there. When that part is facing away from the Sun it is night-time. Is the Earth facing the Sun or facing away from it where you are?

◄ If you were in space and looked at the Earth from the side, it would appear to move from left to right. If you looked down on Earth from the North Pole, it would seem to be moving anticlockwise.

8 **The Earth spins around its Poles.** The Earth spins around two points on its surface. They are at opposite ends of the Earth. One is on top of the Earth. It is called the North Pole. The other is at the bottom of the Earth. It is called the South Pole. The North and South Poles are so cold, they are covered by ice and snow.

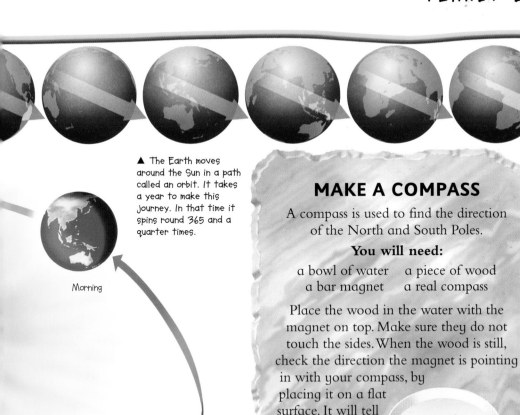

▲ The Earth moves around the Sun in a path called an orbit. It takes a year to make this journey. In that time it spins round 365 and a quarter times.

Morning

Night

▲ As one part of the Earth turns into sunlight, another part turns into darkness. It is morning when a part turns into sunlight, and evening when it turns into darkness.

MAKE A COMPASS

A compass is used to find the direction of the North and South Poles.

You will need:

a bowl of water   a piece of wood
a bar magnet   a real compass

Place the wood in the water with the magnet on top. Make sure they do not touch the sides. When the wood is still, check the direction the magnet is pointing in with your compass, by placing it on a flat surface. It will tell you the direction of the North and South Poles.

9 The spinning Earth acts like a magnet. At the centre of the Earth is liquid iron. As the Earth spins, it makes the iron behave like a magnet with a North and South Pole. These act on the magnet in a compass to make the needle point to the North and South Poles.

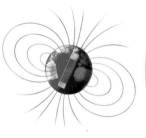

▲ These lines show the pulling power of the magnet inside the Earth.

13

Inside the Earth

10 **There are different parts to the Earth.** There is a thin, rocky crust, a solid middle called the mantle and a centre called the core. The outer part of the core is liquid but the inner core is made of solid metal.

11 **At the centre of the Earth is a huge metal ball called the inner core.** It is 2500 kilometres wide and is made mainly from iron, with some nickel. The ball has an incredible temperature of 6000°C – hot enough to make the metals melt. They stay solid because other parts of the Earth push down heavily on them.

12 **Around the centre of the Earth flows a hot, liquid layer of iron and nickel.** This layer is the outer core and is about 2200 kilometres thick. As the Earth spins, the metal ball and liquid layer move at different speeds.

Crust

Mantle
4500°C

Outer core
6000°C

Inner core
7000°C

◀ The internal structure of the Earth. The centre of the Earth – the inner core – is solid even though it is intensely hot. This is because it is under extreme pressure.

13 The largest part of Earth is a layer called the mantle, which is 2900 kilometres thick. It lies between the core and the crust. Near the crust, the mantle is made of slow-moving rock. When you squeeze an open tube of toothpaste, the toothpaste moves a little like the rocks in the upper mantle.

300 million years ago

200 million years ago

14 The Earth's surface is covered by crust. Land is made of continental crust between 20 and 70 kilometres thick. Most of this is made from a rock called granite. The ocean bed is made of oceanic crust about eight kilometres thick. It is made mainly from a rock called basalt.

▶ Scientists know that the continents were once joined because matching rocks and fossils are found in places that are now separated by vast oceans.

65 million years ago

15 The crust is divided into huge slabs of rock called plates. Most plates have land and seas on top of them but some, like the Pacific Plate, are mostly covered by water. The large areas of land on the plates are called continents. There are seven continents – Africa, Asia, Europe, North America, South America, Oceania and Antarctica.

16 Very, very slowly, the continents are moving. Slow-flowing mantle under the crust moves the plates across the Earth's surface. As the plates move, so do the continents. In some places, the plates push into each other. In others, they move apart. North America is moving three centimetres away from Europe every year!

Hot rocks

17 There are places on Earth where hot, liquid rocks shoot up through its surface. These are volcanoes. Beneath a volcano is a huge space filled with molten (liquid) rock. This is the magma chamber. Inside the chamber, pressure builds like the pressure in a fizzy drink's can if you shake it. Ash, steam and molten rock called lava escape from the top of the volcano – this is an eruption.

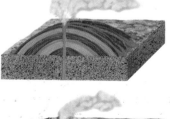

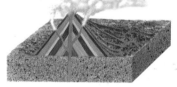

▲ These volcanoes are a shield volcano (top), a crater volcano (middle) and a cone-shaped volcano (bottom).

18 Volcanoes erupt in different ways and have different shapes. Most have a central tube called a pipe, reaching up to the vent opening. Some volcanoes have runny lava, like those in Hawaii. It flows from the vent and makes a domed shape called a shield volcano. Other volcanoes have thick lava. When they erupt, gases in the lava make it explode into pieces of ash. The ash settles on the lava to make a cone-shaped volcano. A caldera, or crater volcano, is made when the top of a cone-shaped volcano explodes and sinks into the magma chamber.

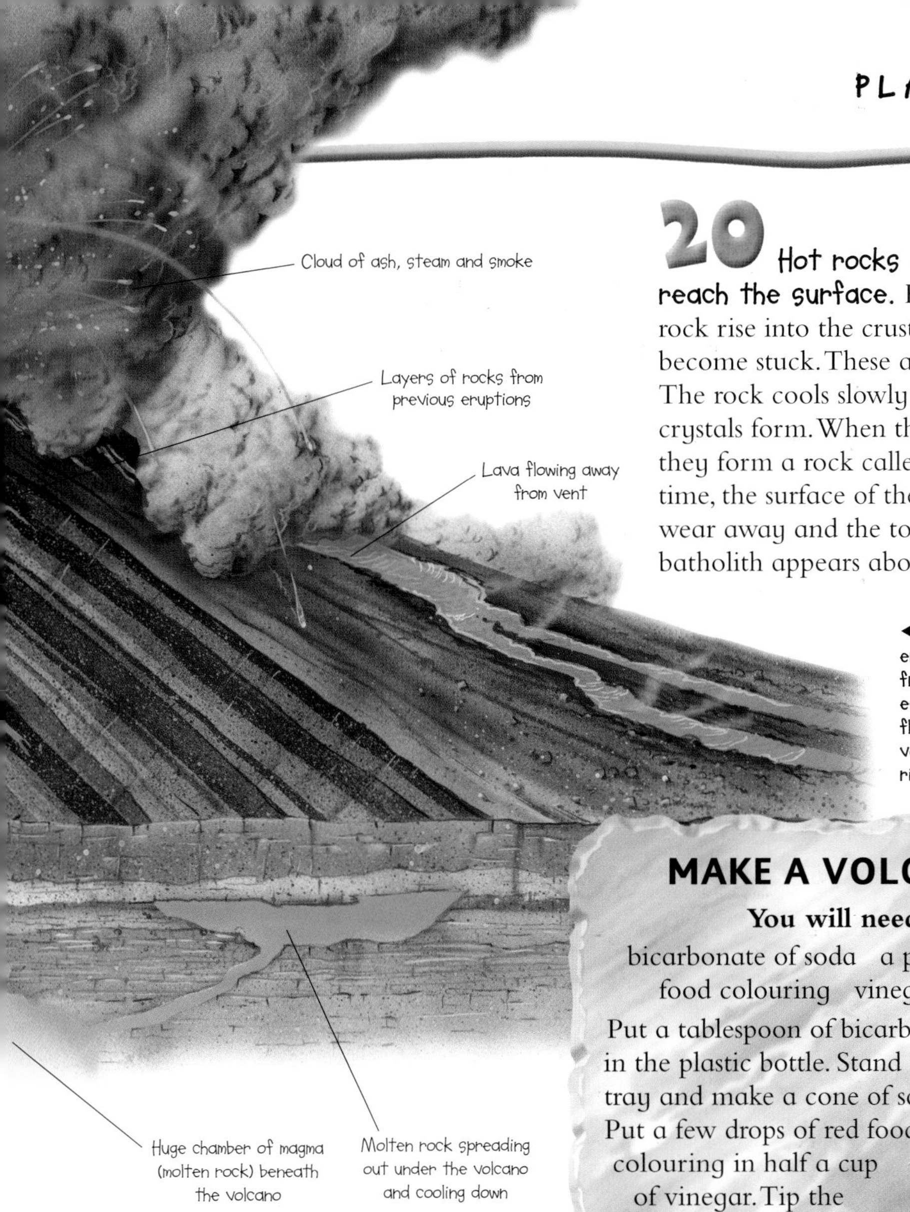

Cloud of ash, steam and smoke

Layers of rocks from previous eruptions

Lava flowing away from vent

20 **Hot rocks don't always reach the surface.** Huge lumps of rock rise into the crust and can become stuck. These are batholiths. The rock cools slowly and large crystals form. When the crystals cool, they form a rock called granite. In time, the surface of the crust may wear away and the top of the batholith appears above ground.

◀ When a volcano erupts, the hot rock from inside the Earth escapes as ash, smoke, flying lumps called volcanic bombs and rivers of lava.

Huge chamber of magma (molten rock) beneath the volcano

Molten rock spreading out under the volcano and cooling down

MAKE A VOLCANO
You will need:
bicarbonate of soda   a plastic bottle
food colouring   vinegar   sand

Put a tablespoon of bicarbonate of soda in the plastic bottle. Stand the bottle in a tray and make a cone of sand around it. Put a few drops of red food colouring in half a cup of vinegar. Tip the vinegar into a jug then pour it into the bottle. In a few moments the volcano should erupt with red, frothy lava.

19 **There are volcanoes under the sea.** Where plates in the crust move apart, lava flows out from rift volcanoes to fill the gap. The hot lava is cooled quickly by the sea and forms pillow-shaped lumps called pillow lava.

Boil and bubble

21 **A geyser can be found on top of some old volcanoes.** If these volcanoes collapse, their rocks settle above hot rocks in the old magma chamber. The gaps between the broken rocks make a group of pipes and chambers. Rainwater seeps in, collecting in the chambers, where it is heated until it boils. Steam builds up, pushing the water through the pipes and out of a cone-shaped opening called a nozzle. Steam and water shoot through the nozzle, making a fountain up to 60 metres high.

▲ Geysers are common in the volcanic regions of New Zealand in Oceania. In some areas they are even used to help make electricity.

22 **In the ocean are hot springs called black smokers.** They form near rift volcanoes, where water is heated by the volcanoes' magma chambers. The hot water dissolves chemicals in the rocks, which turn black when they are cooled by the surrounding ocean water. They rise like clouds of smoke from chimneys.

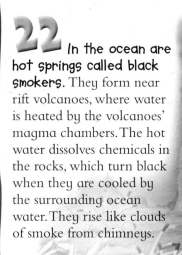

23 **In a hot spring, the water bubbles gently to the surface.** As the water is heated in the chamber, it rises up a pipe and into a pool. The pool may be brightly coloured due to tiny plants and animals called algae and bacteria. These live in large numbers in the hot water.

◄ The chimneys of a black smoker are made by chemicals in the hot water. These stick together to form a rocky pipe.

24 Wallowing in a mud pot can make your skin soft and smooth. A mud pot is made when fumes break down rocks into tiny pieces. These mix with water to make mud. Hot fumes push through the mud, making it bubble. Some mud pots are cool enough to wallow in.

Mud pot

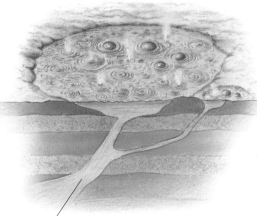

Very hot water mixes with mud at the surface

▲ The bubbles in a mud pot grow as they fill with fumes. Eventually they pop and the fumes escape into the air.

26 In Iceland, underground steam is used to make lights work. The steam is sent to power stations and is used to work generators to make electricity. The electricity then flows to homes and powers electrical equipment such as lights, televisions and computers.

25 Steam and smelly fumes can escape from holes in the ground. These holes are called fumaroles. Since Roman times, people have used the steam from fumaroles for steam baths. The steam may keep joints and lungs healthy.

Fumarole   Released steam

Very hot water

▲ Under a fumarole the water gets so hot that it turns to steam, then shoots upwards into the air.

MAKE A GEYSER

You will need:
a bucket   a plastic funnel
plastic tubing

Fill a bucket with water. Turn the plastic funnel upside down and sink most of it in the water. Take a piece of plastic tube and put one end under the funnel. Blow down the other end of the tube. A spray of water and air will shoot out of the funnel. Be prepared for a wet face!

Breaking down rocks

27 Ice has the power to make rocks crumble. In cold weather, rainwater gets into cracks in rocks and freezes. Water swells as it turns to ice. The ice pushes with such power on the rock that it opens up the cracks. Over a long time, a rock can be broken down into thousands of tiny pieces.

▲ In cold climates, water in cracks in the rock turns to ice, forcing the layers apart and fragments are broken off.

28 Living things can break down rocks. Sometimes a tree seed lands in a crack in a rock. In time, a tree grows and its large roots smash open the rock. Tiny living things called lichens dissolve the surface of rocks to reach minerals they need to live. When animals, such as rabbits, make a burrow they may break up some of the rock in the ground.

▲ Tree roots grow into joints in many rocks. As the roots get larger, the rock is forced apart.

29 Warming up and cooling down can break rocks into flakes. When a rock warms up it swells a little. When it cools, the rock shrinks back to its original size. After swelling and shrinking many times some rocks break up into flakes. Sometimes layers of large flakes form on a rock and make it look like onion skin.

▶ When rocks are heated and cooled in deserts, flakes of rock break off unevenly and make patterns of ridges on the rock surface.

30

Glaciers break up rocks and carry them away. Glaciers are huge areas of ice which form near mountain tops. They slide slowly down the mountainside and melt. As a glacier moves, some rocks are snapped off and carried along. Others are ground up and carried along as grit and sand.

▶ Snow falls on mountain tops and squashes down to make ice. The ice forms the glacier which slowly moves down the mountainside until it melts.

Region where glacier forms

Moving ice

Where the glacier melts is called the snout

31

Rocks in rivers and seas are always getting smaller. Water flows over rocks, gradually wearing them down. The water also dissolves minerals from the rock. As well as this, sand and grit in the water slowly grind away the rock surfaces.

I DON'T BELIEVE IT!

In one part of Turkey, people have cut caves in huge cones of rock to make homes.

32

Wind can blow a rock to pieces, but it takes a long time. Strong winds hurl dust and sand grains at a rock, which slowly blast pieces from its surface. It then blows away any tiny loose chips that have formed on the surface of the rock.

Arch

Settling down

33 **Stones of different sizes can stick together to make rock.** Thousands of years ago, boulders, pebbles and gravel settled on the shores of seas and lakes. These have become stuck together to make a rock called conglomerate. At the foot of cliffs, broken, rocky pieces collected and stuck together to make a rock called breccia. The lumps in breccia have sharp edges.

▲ Pieces of rock can become stuck together by a natural cement to make a lump of larger rock, such as breccia

▲ Natural cement binds grains of sand together to make sandstone.

34 **Sandstone can be made in the sea or in the desert.** When a thick layer of sand builds up, the grains are pressed together and cement forms. This sticks the grains together to make sandstone. Sea sandstone may be yellow with sharp-edged grains. Desert sandstone may be red with round, smooth grains.

35 **If mud is squashed hard enough, it turns to stone.** Mud is made from tiny particles of clay and slightly larger particles called silt. When huge layers of mud formed in ancient rivers, lakes and seas, they were squashed by their own weight to make mudstone.

▶ Mudstone has a very smooth surface. It may be grey, black, brown or yellow.

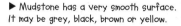

36
Limestone is made from sea shells. Many kinds of sea animal have a hard shell. When the animal dies, the shell remains on the sea floor. In time, large numbers of shells build up and press together to form limestone. Huge numbers of shells become fossils.

► Limestone is usually white, cream, grey or yellow. Caves often form in areas of limestone.

SEE ROCK SETTLE

You will need:

sand   clay   gravel
a plastic bottle

Put a tablespoon of sand, clay and gravel into a bowl. Mix up the gravel with two cups of water then pour into a plastic bottle. You should see the bits of gravel settle in layers, with the smallest pieces at the bottom and the largest at the top.

37
Chalk is made from millions of shells and the remains of tiny sea creatures. A drop of sea water contains many microscopic organisms (living things). Some of these organisms have shells full of holes. When these organisms die, the shells sink to the sea bed and in time form chalk.

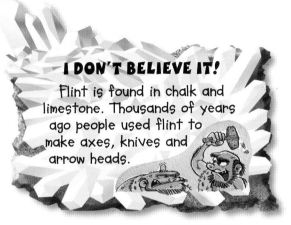

I DON'T BELIEVE IT!
Flint is found in chalk and limestone. Thousands of years ago people used flint to make axes, knives and arrow heads.

▲ Most chalk formed at the time of the dinosaurs, but chalk is forming in some places on the Earth today.

Uncovering fossils

38 **The best fossils formed from animals and plants that were buried quickly.** When a plant or animal dies, it is usually eaten by other living things so that nothing remains. If the plant or animal was buried quickly after death, or even buried alive, its body may be preserved.

▶ This is a fossil skull of *Tyrannosaurus rex*, a dinosaur that roamed the Earth around 70–65 million years ago.

39 **A fossil is made from minerals.** A dead plant or animal can be dissolved by water. An empty space in the shape of the plant or animal is left in the mud and fills with minerals from the surrounding rock. Sometimes, the minerals simply settle in the body, making it harder and heavier.

1. The trilobite lives on the ocean floor

2. The trilobite dies

3. The trilobite is covered by mud

4. The mud turns to stone

5. The fossil forms inside the stone

▲ Many fossils of trilobites, small ocean-dwelling creatures, have been found.

▶ When this ammonite was alive, tentacles would have stuck out of the uncoiled end of the shell.

40 **Some fossils look like coiled snakes but are really shellfish.** These are ammonites. An ammonite's body was covered by a spiral shell. The body rotted away leaving the shell to become the fossil. Ammonites lived in the seas at the same time as the dinosaurs lived on land.

41 Dinosaurs did not just leave fossil bones. Some left whole skeletons behind while others are known from only a few bones. Fossilized teeth, skin, eggs and droppings have been found. When dinosaurs walked across mud they left tracks behind that became fossils. By looking at these, scientists have discovered how dinosaurs walked and how fast they could run.

42 Electricity in your home may have been made by burning fossils. About 300 million years ago the land was covered by forests and swamps. When plants died they fell into the swamps and did not rot away. Over time, their remains were squashed and heated so much that they turned to coal. Today, coal is used to work generators that make electricity.

I DON'T BELIEVE IT!

Some fossils of bacteria are three and a half billion years old.

▶ Coal was formed by trees and plants growing near water. When the trees died the waterlogged ground stopped them rotting away, and peat formed.

Dead trees are buried and squashed to form peat

The peat hardens to form coal

Rocks that change

43 **When a rock forms in the crust it may soon be changed again.** There are two main ways this can happen. In one way, the rock is heated by hot rocks moving up through the crust. In another way the crust is squashed and heated as mountains form. Both of these ways make crystals in the rock change to form new types of rocks.

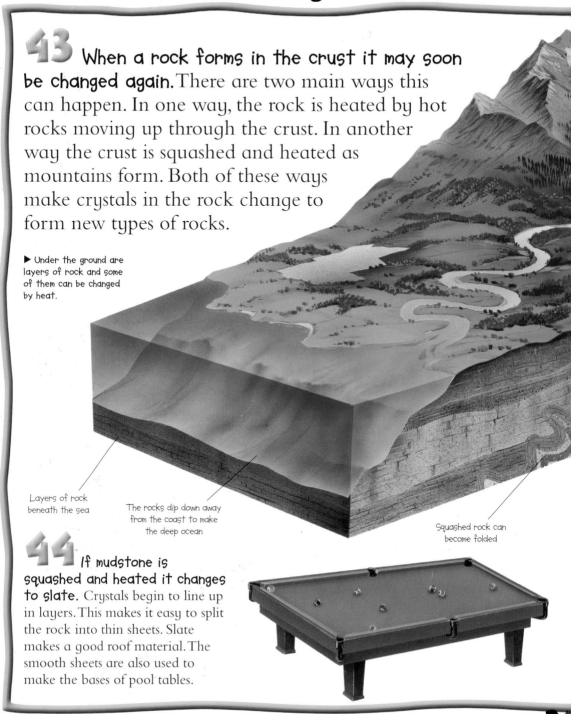

▶ Under the ground are layers of rock and some of them can be changed by heat.

Layers of rock beneath the sea

The rocks dip down away from the coast to make the deep ocean

Squashed rock can become folded

44 **If mudstone is squashed and heated it changes to slate.** Crystals begin to line up in layers. This makes it easy to split the rock into thin sheets. Slate makes a good roof material. The smooth sheets are also used to make the bases of pool tables.

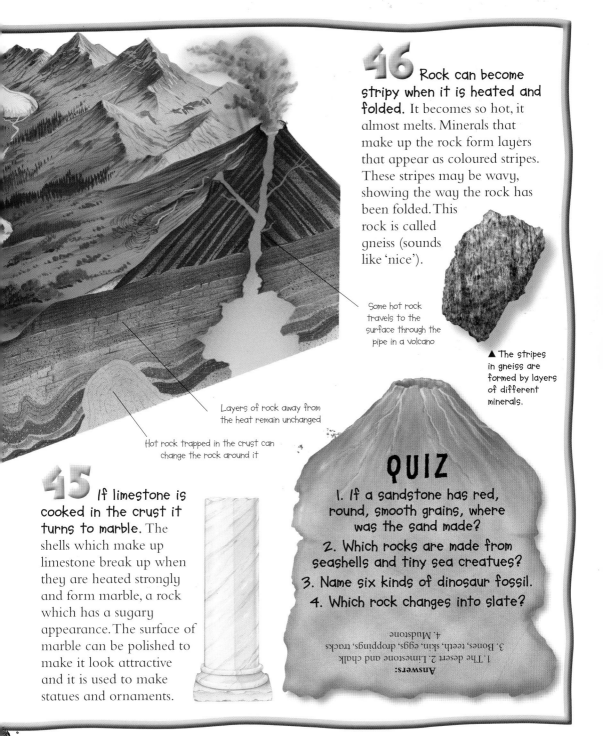

46 Rock can become stripy when it is heated and folded. It becomes so hot, it almost melts. Minerals that make up the rock form layers that appear as coloured stripes. These stripes may be wavy, showing the way the rock has been folded. This rock is called gneiss (sounds like 'nice').

Some hot rock travels to the surface through the pipe in a volcano

▲ The stripes in gneiss are formed by layers of different minerals.

Layers of rock away from the heat remain unchanged

Hot rock trapped in the crust can change the rock around it

45 If limestone is cooked in the crust it turns to marble. The shells which make up limestone break up when they are heated strongly and form marble, a rock which has a sugary appearance. The surface of marble can be polished to make it look attractive and it is used to make statues and ornaments.

QUIZ
1. If a sandstone has red, round, smooth grains, where was the sand made?
2. Which rocks are made from seashells and tiny sea creatues?
3. Name six kinds of dinosaur fossil.
4. Which rock changes into slate?

Answers:
1. The desert 2. Limestone and chalk
3. Bones, teeth, skin, eggs, droppings, tracks
4. Mudstone

Massive mountains

47 The youngest mountains on Earth are the highest. Highest of all is Mount Everest, which formed 15 million years ago. Young mountains have jagged peaks because softer rocks on the mountain top are broken down by the weather. These pointy peaks are made from harder rocks that take longer to break down. In time, even these hard rocks are worn away. This makes an older mountain shorter and gives its top a rounded shape.

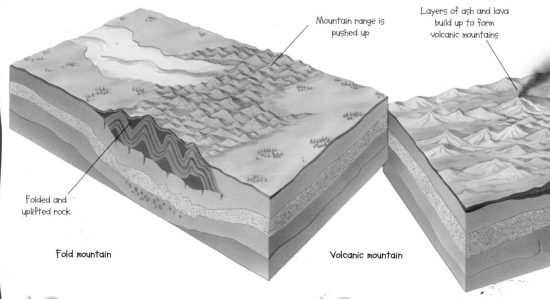

Mountain range is pushed up

Layers of ash and lava build up to form volcanic mountains

Folded and uplifted rock

Fold mountain

Volcanic mountain

48 When plates in the Earth's crust crash together, mountains are formed. When two continental plates crash together, the crust at the edge of the plates crumples and folds, pushing up ranges of mountains. The Himalayan Mountains in Asia formed in this way.

49 Some of the Earth's highest mountains are volcanoes. These are formed when molten rock (lava) erupts through the Earth's crust. As the lava cools, it forms a rocky layer. With each new eruption, another layer is added.

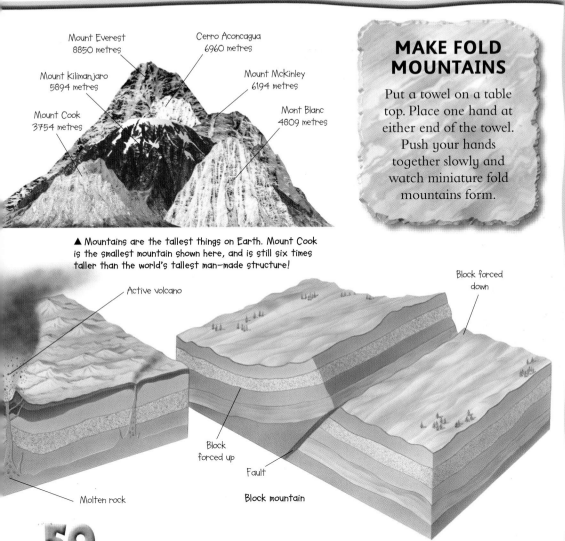

Mount Everest
8850 metres

Cerro Aconcagua
6960 metres

Mount Kilimanjaro
5894 metres

Mount McKinley
6194 metres

Mount Cook
3754 metres

Mont Blanc
4809 metres

▲ Mountains are the tallest things on Earth. Mount Cook is the smallest mountain shown here, and is still six times taller than the world's tallest man-made structure!

Active volcano

Block forced down

Block forced up

Fault

Molten rock

Block mountain

MAKE FOLD MOUNTAINS

Put a towel on a table top. Place one hand at either end of the towel. Push your hands together slowly and watch miniature fold mountains form.

50 The movement of the Earth's crust can make blocks of rock pop up to make mountains. When the plates in the crust push together, they make heat which softens the rock, letting it fold. Farther away from this heat, cooler rock snaps when it is pushed. The snapped rock makes huge cracks called faults in the crust. When a block of rock between two faults is pushed by the rest of the crust, it rises to form a block mountain.

▲ It takes millions of years for mountains to form and the process is happening all the time. A group of mountains is called a range. The biggest ranges are the Alps in Europe, the Andes in South America, the Rockies in North America and the highest of all – the Himalayas in Asia.

Shaking the Earth

51 **An earthquake is caused by violent movements in the Earth's crust.** Most occur when two plates in the crust rub together. An earthquake starts deep underground at its 'focus'. Shock waves move from the focus in all directions, shaking the rock. Where the shock waves reach the surface is called the epicentre. This is where the greatest shaking occurs.

52 **The power of an earthquake can vary.** Half a million earthquakes happen every year but hardly any can be felt by people. About 25 earthquakes each year are powerful enough to cause disasters. Earthquake strength is measured by the Richter Scale. The higher the number, the more destructive the earthquake.

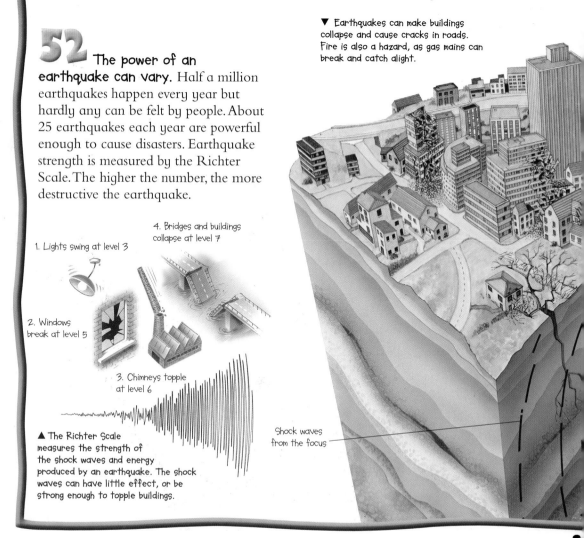

▼ Earthquakes can make buildings collapse and cause cracks in roads. Fire is also a hazard, as gas mains can break and catch alight.

1. Lights swing at level 3

2. Windows break at level 5

3. Chimneys topple at level 6

4. Bridges and buildings collapse at level 7

▲ The Richter Scale measures the strength of the shock waves and energy produced by an earthquake. The shock waves can have little effect, or be strong enough to topple buildings.

Shock waves from the focus

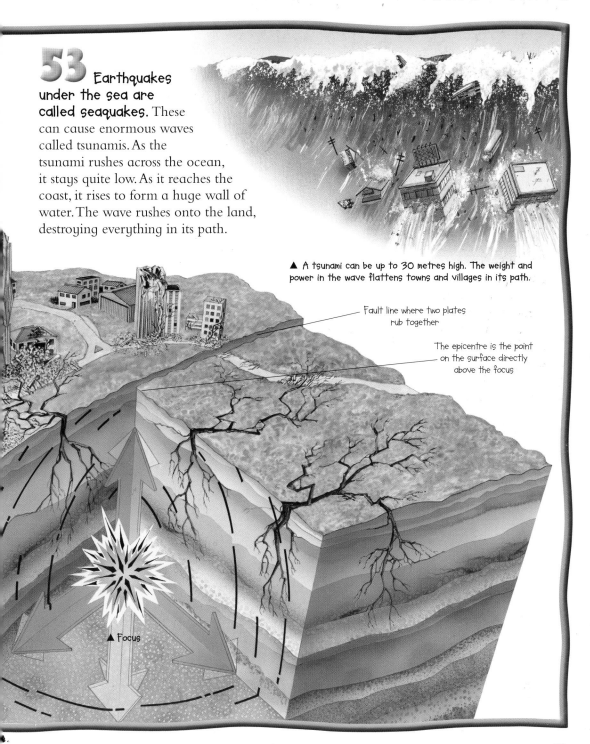

53 Earthquakes under the sea are called seaquakes. These can cause enormous waves called tsunamis. As the tsunami rushes across the ocean, it stays quite low. As it reaches the coast, it rises to form a huge wall of water. The wave rushes onto the land, destroying everything in its path.

▲ A tsunami can be up to 30 metres high. The weight and power in the wave flattens towns and villages in its path.

Fault line where two plates rub together

The epicentre is the point on the surface directly above the focus

▲ Focus

Cavernous caves

54 **Some caves are made from a tube of lava.** As lava moves down the side of a volcano, its surface cools down quickly. The cold lava becomes solid but below, the lava remains warm and keeps on flowing. Under the solid surface a tube may form in which liquid lava flows. When the tube empties, a cave is formed.

▲ A cave made by lava is so large that people can walk through it without having to bend down.

Waterfall in a shaft

Waterfall in a sink hole

1. Water seeps through cracks in rock

55 **When rain falls on limestone it becomes a cave-maker.** Rainwater can mix with carbon dioxide to form an acid strong enough to attack limestone and make it dissolve. Underground, the action of the rainwater makes caves in which streams and lakes can be found.

▶ Water runs through the caves in limestone rock and makes pools and streams. In wet weather it may flood the caves.

2. Underground stream carves into rock

▼ Water flows through the cracks in limestone and makes them wider to form caves. The horizontal caves are called galleries and the vertical caves are called shafts.

3. Large cave system develops

Gallery

Cave opening

I DON'T BELIEVE IT!

The longest stalactite is 59 metres long. The tallest stalagmite is 32 metres tall.

56 **Dripping water in a limestone cave makes rock spikes.** When water drips from a cave roof it leaves a small piece of limestone behind. A small spike of rock begins to form. This rock spike, called a stalactite, may grow from the ceiling. Where the drops splash onto the cave floor, tiny pieces of limestone gather. They form a spike which points upwards. This is a stalagmite. Over long periods of time, the two spikes may join together to form a column of rock.

The Earth's treasure

57 Gold may form small grains, large nuggets or veins in the rocks. When the rocks wear away, the grains may be found in the sand of river beds. Silver forms branching wires in rock. It does not shine like jewellery but is covered in a black coating called tarnish.

▲ Gold nuggets like this one can be melted and moulded to form all kinds of jewellery.

58 Most metals are found in rocks called ores. An ore is a mixture of different substances, of which metal is one. Each metal has its own ore. For example, aluminium is found in a yellow ore called bauxite. Heat is used to get metals from their ores. We use metals to make thousands of different things, ranging from watches to jumbo jets.

◄ Silver is used for making jewellery and ornaments.

59 Beautiful crystals can grow in lava bubbles. Lava contains gases which form bubbles. When the lava cools and becomes solid, the bubbles form balloon-shaped spaces in the rock. These are called geodes. Liquids seep into them and form large crystals. The gemstone amethyst forms in this way.

► Inside a geode there is space for crystals, such as amethyst crystals, to spread out, grow and form perfect shapes.

▲ This is bauxite, the ore of aluminium. Heat, chemicals and electricity are used to get the metal out of the rock. Aluminium is used to make all kinds of things, from kitchen foil to aeroplanes.

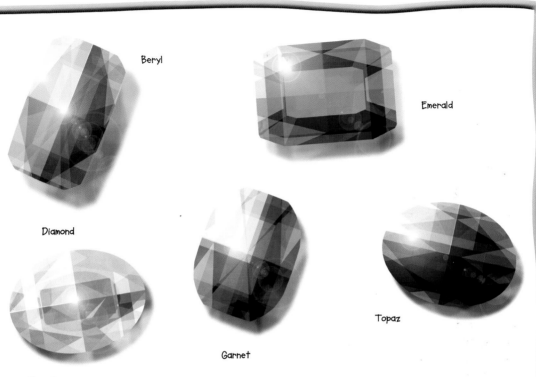

Beryl

Emerald

Diamond

Topaz

Garnet

▲ There are more than 100 different kinds of gemstone. Some are associated with different months of the year and are known as 'birthstones'. For example, the birthstone for September is sapphire.

60 Gemstones are coloured rocks which are cut and polished to make them sparkle. People have used them to make jewellery for thousands of years. Gems such as topaz, emerald and garnet formed in hot rocks which rose to the Earth's crust and cooled. Most are found as small crystals, but a gem called beryl can have a huge crystal – the largest ever found was 18 metres long! Diamond is a gemstone and is the hardest natural substance found on Earth.

MAKE CRYSTALS FROM SALT WATER

You will need:

table salt
a magnifying glass
a dark-coloured bowl

Dissolve some table salt in some warm water. Pour the salty water into a dark-coloured bowl. Put the bowl in a warm place so the water can evaporate. After a few days, you can look at the crystals with a magnifying glass.

Wild weather

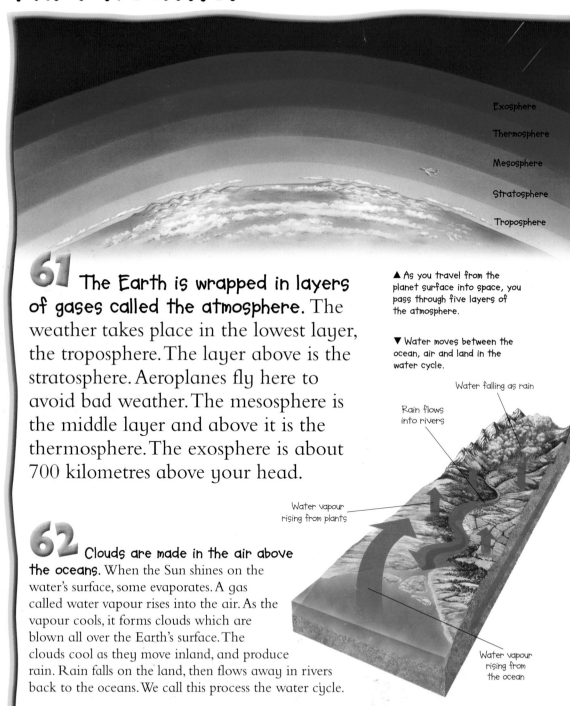

Exosphere

Thermosphere

Mesosphere

Stratosphere

Troposphere

61 **The Earth is wrapped in layers of gases called the atmosphere.** The weather takes place in the lowest layer, the troposphere. The layer above is the stratosphere. Aeroplanes fly here to avoid bad weather. The mesosphere is the middle layer and above it is the thermosphere. The exosphere is about 700 kilometres above your head.

▲ As you travel from the planet surface into space, you pass through five layers of the atmosphere.

▼ Water moves between the ocean, air and land in the water cycle.

Water falling as rain

Rain flows into rivers

Water vapour rising from plants

Water vapour rising from the ocean

62 **Clouds are made in the air above the oceans.** When the Sun shines on the water's surface, some evaporates. A gas called water vapour rises into the air. As the vapour cools, it forms clouds which are blown all over the Earth's surface. The clouds cool as they move inland, and produce rain. Rain falls on the land, then flows away in rivers back to the oceans. We call this process the water cycle.

▶ A hurricane forms over the surface of a warm ocean but it can move to the coast and onto the land.

63 **A hurricane is a destructive storm which gathers over a warm part of the ocean.** Water evaporating from the ocean forms a vast cloud. As cool air rushes in below the cloud, it turns like a huge spinning wheel. The centre of the hurricane (the eye) is completely still. But all around, winds gust at speeds of 300 kilometres an hour. If it reaches land the hurricane can blow buildings to pieces.

65 **Snowflakes form in the tops of clouds.** It is so cold here that water freezes to make ice crystals. As the snowflakes get larger, they fall through the cloud. If the cloud is in warm air, the snowflakes melt and form raindrops. If the cloud is in cold air, the snowflakes reach the ground and begin to settle.

▼ The ice crystals in a snowflake usually form six arms.

64 **A tornado is the fastest wind on Earth — it can spin at speeds of 500 kilometres an hour.** Tornadoes form over ground that has become very warm. Fast-rising air makes a spinning funnel which acts as a vacuum cleaner. It can devastate buildings and lift up cars and traffic, flinging them to the ground.

I DON'T BELIEVE IT!
Every day there are 45,000 thunderstorms on the Earth.

Lands of sand and grass

66 **The driest places on Earth are deserts.** In many deserts there is a short period of rain every year, but some deserts have dry weather for many years. The main deserts of the world are shown on the map.

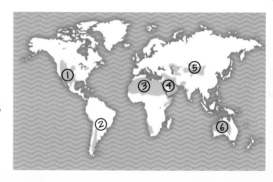

▲ This map shows the major deserts of the world. ① North American deserts – Great Basin and Mojave ② Atacama ③ Sahara ④ Arabian ⑤ Gobi ⑥ Australian deserts – Great Sandy, Gibson, Great Victoria, Simpson.

67 **Deserts are not always hot.** It can be as hot as 50°C in the day-time but at night the temperature falls quickly. Deserts near the Equator have hot days all year round but some deserts farther from the Equator have very cold winters.

Ridges of sand being blown into dunes

Barchan dune

Rock beneath the desert

I DON'T BELIEVE IT!

The camel has broad feet that stop it sinking in the sand.

68 **Sand dunes are made by the winds blowing across a desert.** If there is only a small amount of sand on the desert floor, the wind blows crescent-shaped dunes called barchans. If there is plenty of sand, it forms long, straight dunes called transverse dunes. If the wind blows in two directions, it makes long wavy dunes called seif dunes.

69
An oasis is a pool of water in the desert. It forms from rainwater that has seeped into the sand then collected in rock. The water then moves through the rock to where the sand is very thin and forms a pool. Trees and plants grow around the pool and animals visit the pool to drink.

▼ Plants and animals can thrive at an oasis in the middle of a desert.

Oasis

70
A desert cactus stores water in its stem. The grooves on the stem let it swell with water to keep the plant alive in dry weather. The spines stop animals biting into the cactus for a drink.

71
Grasslands are found where there is too much rain for a desert and not enough rain for a forest. Tropical grasslands near the Equator are hot all year round. Grasslands farther from the Equator have warm summers and cool winters.

72
Large numbers of animals live on grasslands. In Africa zebras feed on the top of grass stalks, gnu feed on the middle leaves and gazelles feed on the new shoots. This allows all the animals to feed together. Other animals such as lions feed on plant eaters.

▼ Three types of animals can live together by eating plants of different heights. Zebras ① eat the tall grass. Gnu ② eat the middle shoots and gazelle ③ browse on the lowest shoots.

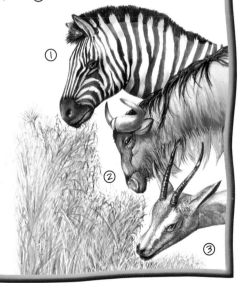

①

②

③

Fantastic forests

73 **There are three main kinds of forest.** They are coniferous, temperate and tropical forests. The main forest regions are shown on the world map opposite.

▲ This map shows the major areas of forest in the world:
① Coniferous forest ② Temperate forest
③ Tropical forest

74 **Coniferous trees form huge forests around the northern part of the planet.** They have long, green, needle-like leaves covered in wax. These trees stay in leaf throughout the year. In winter, the wax helps snow slide off the leaves so that sunlight can reach them to keep them alive. Coniferous trees produce seeds in cones. These are eaten by squirrels.

76 Large numbers of huge trees grow close together in a rainforest. They have broad, evergreen leaves and branches that almost touch. These form a leafy roof over the forest called a canopy. It rains almost every day in a rainforest and the vegetation is so thick, it can take a raindrop ten minutes to fall to the ground. Three-quarters of all known species of animals and plants live in rainforests. They include huge hairy spiders, brightly coloured frogs and spotted jungle cats.

75 Most trees in temperate forests have flat, broad leaves and need large amounts of water to keep them alive. In winter, the trees cannot get enough water from the frozen ground, so they lose their leaves and grow new ones in spring. Deer, rabbits, foxes and mice live on the woodland floor while squirrels, woodpeckers and owls live in the trees.

QUIZ

1. What forms at the top of a cloud?

2. What shape is a barchan sand dune?

3. In which kind of forest would you find brightly coloured frogs?

Answers:
1. Snow flake 2. Crescent
3. Tropical

41

Rivers and lakes

77 **A mighty river can start from a spring.** This is a place where water flows from the ground. Rain soaks into the ground, through the soil and rock, until it gushes out on the side of a hill. The trickle of water from a spring is called a stream. Many streams join together to make a river.

78 **Water wears rocks down to make a waterfall.** When a river flows off a layer of hard rock onto softer rock, it wears the softer rock away. The rocks and pebbles in the water grind the soft rock away to make a cliff face. At the bottom of the waterfall they make a deep pool called a plunge pool.

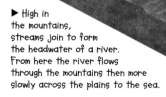

Oxbow lake

Meander

Delta

▶ High in the mountains, streams join to form the headwater of a river. From here the river flows through the mountains then more slowly across the plains to the sea.

79 **A river changes as it flows to the sea.** Rivers begin in hills and mountains. They are narrow and flow quickly there. When the river flows through flatter land it becomes wider and slow-moving. It makes loops called meanders which may separate and form oxbow lakes. Where the river meets the sea is the river mouth. It may be a wide channel called an estuary or a group of sandy islands called a delta.

◀ Waterfalls may only be a few centimetres high, or come crashing over a cliff with a massive drop. Angel Falls in Venezuela form the highest falls in the world. One of the drops is an amazing 807 metres.

Headwater

80 **Lakes form in hollows in the ground.** The hollows may be left when glaciers melt or when plates in the crust split open. Some lakes form when a landslide makes a dam across a river.

▲ A landslide has fallen into the river and blocked the flow of water to make a lake.

▼ A volcano can sometimes form in a lake inside a crater.

81 **A lake can form in the crater of a volcano.** A few crater lakes have formed in craters left by meteorites that hit Earth long ago.

▼ Most lakes are just blue but some are green, pink, red or even white. The Laguna Colorado in Chile is red due to tiny organisms (creatures) that live in the water.

82 **Some lake water may be brightly coloured.** The colours are made by tiny organisms called algae or by minerals dissolved in the water.

43

World of water

83 **There is so much water on our planet that it could be called 'Ocean' instead of Earth.** Only about one third of the planet is covered by land. The rest is covered by four huge areas of water called oceans. A sea is a smaller area of water in an ocean. For example the North Sea is part of the Atlantic Ocean and the Malayan Sea is part of the Pacific Ocean.

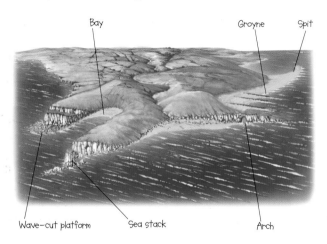

Bay
Groyne
Spit
Wave-cut platform
Sea stack
Arch

84 **Coasts are always changing.** Where the sea and land meet is called the coast. In many places waves crash onto the land and break it up. Caves and arches are punched into cliffs. In time, the arches break and leave columns of rock called sea stacks.

◀ The rocks at the coast are broken up by the action of the waves.

Continental shelf
Continental slope

85 **The oceans are so deep that mountains are hidden beneath them.** If you paddle by the shore, sea water is quite shallow. Out in the ocean it can be up to eight kilometres deep. The ocean floor is a flat plain with mountain ranges rising across it. They mark where two places in the crust meet. Nearer the coast may be deep trenches where the edges of two plates have moved apart. Extinct volcanoes form mountains called sea mounts.

▲ Corals only grow in tropical or sub-tropical waters. They tend to grow in shallow water where there is lots of sunlight.

87 There are thousands of icebergs floating in the oceans. They are made from glaciers and ice sheets which have formed at the North and South Poles. Only about a tenth of an iceberg can be seen above water. The rest lies below and can sink ships that sail too close.

▶ Under every iceberg is a huge amount of ice, usually much bigger than the area visible from the surface.

86 Tiny creatures can make islands in the oceans. Coral have jelly-like bodies and they live together in their millions. They make rocky homes from minerals in sea water that protects them from feeding fish. Coral builds up to create islands around extinct volcanoes in the Pacific and Indian Oceans.

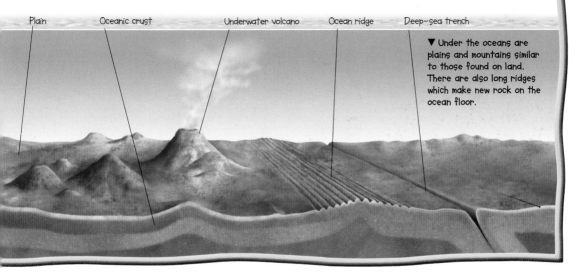

Plain   Oceanic crust   Underwater volcano   Ocean ridge   Deep-sea trench

▼ Under the oceans are plains and mountains similar to those found on land. There are also long ridges which make new rock on the ocean floor.

45

The planet of life

88 **There are millions of different kinds of life forms on Earth.** So far, life has not been found anywhere else. Living things survive here because it is warm, there is water and the air contains oxygen. If we discover other planets with these conditions, there may be life on them too.

89 **Many living things on the Earth are tiny.** They are so small that we cannot see them. A whale shark is the largest fish on the planet, yet it feeds on tiny shrimp-like creatures. These in turn feed on even smaller plant-like organisms called plankton, which make food from sunlight and sea water. Microscopic bacteria are found in the soil and even on your skin.

▲ Despite being the biggest fish in the oceans, the mighty whale shark feeds on tiny shrimp-like creatures and plankton (right).

90 **Animals cannot live without plants.** A plant makes food from sunlight, water, air and minerals in the soil. Animals cannot make their own food so many of them eat plants. Others survive by eating the plant-eaters. If plants died out, all the animals would die too.

◄ This caterpillar eats as much plant-life as possible before beginning its change to a butterfly.

91 The air can be full of animals.
On a warm day, midges and gnats form
clouds close to the ground. In spring and
autumn flocks of birds fly to different parts
of the world to nest. On summer evenings
bats hunt for midges flying in the air.

92 The surface of the ground is
home to many small animals. Mice
scurry through the grass. Larger
animals such as deer hide in
bushes. The elephant is the largest
land animal. It does not need to hide
because few animals would attack it.

93 If you dig into the ground you
can find animals living there. The
earthworm is a common creature found in
the soil. It feeds on rotting plants that it
pulls into the soil. Earthworms are eaten
by moles that dig their way underground.

I DON'T BELIEVE IT!
The star-nosed mole has
feelers on the end
of its nose. It
uses them to
find food.

Caring for the planet

94 **Many useful materials come from the Earth.** These make clothes, buildings, furniture and containers such as cans. Some materials, like those used to make buildings, last a long time. Others, such as those used to make cans, may be used up on the day they are bought.

95 **We may run out of some materials in the future.** Metals are found in rocks called ores. When all the ore has been used up we will not be able to make new metal. Wood is a material that we may not run out of as new trees are always being planted. We must still be careful not to use too much wood, because new trees may not grow fast enough for our needs.

1. Old bottles are collected from bottle banks

2. The glass or plastic are re-cycled to make raw materials

3. The raw materials are re-used to make new bottles

▲ The waste collected at a recycling centre is changed back into useful materials to make many of the things we frequently use.

Exhaust fumes from traffic clog up the atmosphere

96 **We can make materials last longer by recycling them.** Metal, glass and plastic are thrown away after they have been used, buried in tips and never used again. Today more people recycle materials. This means sending them back to factories to be used again.

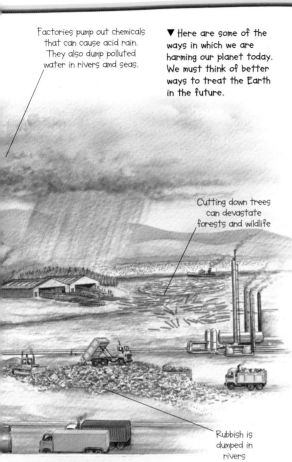

Factories pump out chemicals that can cause acid rain. They also dump polluted water in rivers and seas.

▼ Here are some of the ways in which we are harming our planet today. We must think of better ways to treat the Earth in the future.

Cutting down trees can devastate forests and wildlife

Rubbish is dumped in rivers

98 **Air and water can be polluted by our activities.** Burning coal and oil makes fumes which can make rainwater acidic. This can kill trees and damages soil. When we make materials, chemicals are often released into rivers and seas, endangering wildlife.

99 **Living things can be protected.** Large areas of land have been made into national parks where wildlife is protected. People can come to study both plants and animals.

100 **The Earth is nearly five billion years old.** From a ball of molten rock it has changed into a living, breathing planet. We must try to keep it that way. Switching off lights to save energy and picking up litter are small things we can all do.

97 **We use huge amounts of fuel to make energy.** The main fuels are coal and oil, which are used in power stations to make electricity. Oil is also used in petrol for cars. In time, these fuels will run out. Scientists are trying to develop ways of using other energy sources such as the wind and wave power. Huge windmills are already used to make electricity.

I DON'T BELIEVE IT!
By the middle of the 21st century 30 to 50 percent of all living species may be extinct.

It's cold at the Poles!

101 **The polar regions are found at the top and bottom of the Earth and they are the coldest, windiest places in the world.** Here, the land and sea stay frozen for most of the year, and snow and ice stretch as far as the eye can see. Only a few creatures are tough enough to survive these frozen conditions.

▼ Ice-breakers like the *Apu* have enough power to smash through metre-thick ice in polar seas. They clear the way for following ships, which must keep up because the ice re-freezes in a few hours.

The ends of the Earth

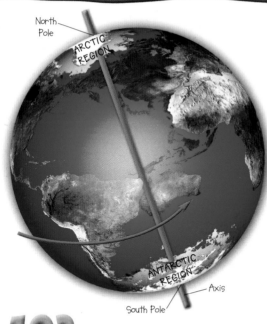

North Pole

ARCTIC REGION

ANTARCTIC REGION

Axis

South Pole

103 **The Earth really has four poles!** There are the Geographic North and South Poles, which are defined by the position of the Earth's axis, but there are also the Magnetic North and South Poles. The Magnetic Poles are some distance from the Geographic Poles.

◀ The Earth spins around an imaginary line called the axis, which passes through the Geographic North and South Poles.

102 **The North and South Poles are at the top and bottom of the Earth.** Every 24 hours, Earth turns once around its axis. The axis is an invisible line that runs through the middle (core) of the Earth, from Pole to Pole.

104 **The Earth is like a giant magnet.** Deep inside the Earth are layers of hot, liquid metals, especially iron. As the Earth turns, the iron moves, creating a magnetic force. The Magnetic Poles are the two places where this force is strongest.

Antarctic Peninsula

105 **Because of the moving liquid metals inside the Earth, the magnetic poles wander, and may move a few metres every year.** Throughout history, the poles have flipped. This is known as magnetic reversal – the Magnetic North Pole becomes the Magnetic South Pole, and the Magnetic South Pole becomes the Magnetic North Pole. The last flip was about 780,000 years ago.

Lines of magnetic force

◀ These lines show the pulling power of the Earth's magnetic core.

▶ The North Pole is in the middle of the Arctic Ocean, which is covered by a floating ice sheet.

ARCTIC OCEAN
(ice sheet)

Geographic North Pole
✳

GREENLAND

106 **The northern polar region is called the Arctic.** The word Arctic comes from the ancient Greek word *arktos*, meaning 'bear'. This refers to the star pattern (constellation) called the Little Bear, or *Ursa Minor*. It contains a star near the North Pole, known as the Pole Star.

Geographic South Pole
✳

ANTARCTICA

◀ ▼ The South Pole is towards one side of the vast, ice-covered land mass of Antarctica. In early April penguins gather at traditonal breeding sites on the sea ice.

I DON'T BELIEVE IT!

Antarctica is the coldest place on Earth. At Vostok Base, the coldest-ever temperature was –89°C in 1983. That's more than four times colder than inside a freezer!

107 **The southern polar region is called the Antarctic.** Ant or anti means 'against' or 'opposite to'. So the Antarctic is simply the region opposite the Arctic, on the other side of the Earth.

SOUTHERN OCEAN

Extreme seasons

108 The Earth's axis is not completely vertical. It is tilted at angle of around 23°. The movement of the Earth around the Sun, combined with this angle, gives our world its seasons.

▲ At the North Pole, the Sun never disappears below the horizon at Midsummer's Day.

109 The Earth moves around (orbits) the Sun. Over the course of a year, first one and then the other Pole leans towards the Sun, giving us seasons.

110 In most polar lands, summer is long and light, and on some days the Sun never sets. Winter is long and dark, and on some days the Sun never rises. The further north or south you are in the world, the more extreme the seasons will be.

▲ Midnight Sun (the presence of the Sun throughout the night), means that people can travel at any time, day or night.

111 When the North Pole is facing away from the Sun, the area around it is in perpetual darkness. The Sun does not rise for at least one night in midwinter. This area is known as the Arctic Circle. The Antarctic Circle is a similar area around the South Pole. When it is midwinter in the Arctic it is midsummer in Antarctica, so at the Antarctic Circle, the Sun does not set for at least one day.

112 Sometimes at night, the polar skies are lit by shimmering, waving curtains of multi-coloured lights. These are called the *Aurora Borealis* or Northern Lights in the Arctic. Around Antarctica they are called the *Aurora Australis* or Southern Lights.

▼ Campers in the forests of the far north see the Northern Lights as a wavy glow. Tonight it is yellow-green. Tomorrow it may be blue or red!

NO SUNSET

You will need:
an apple   a desk lamp

Imagine your apple is the Earth, and the lamp is the Sun. The stem of the apple represents the North Pole. Hold the apple in front of the lamp and angle the stem towards the light. Spin the apple around its core. Despite the spinning, the area around the North Pole has light all the time, while the other side stays in darkness. This illustrates midsummer at the Arctic Circle.

113 The lights are made by tiny particles given off by the Sun, known as the solar wind. These get trapped by the Earth's magnetism and start to glow. This happens very high in the sky, above 100 kilometres, which is three times higher than a passenger jet plane can travel.

Land around a frozen sea

114 The Arctic is a mostly frozen area of the Arctic Ocean that is surrounded by land. The Arctic Ocean is the smallest, shallowest ocean, with an area of about 14 million square kilometres, and an average depth of 1000 metres. During winter, the ice over the ocean becomes up to 3 metres thick. In summer it shrinks, but it never disappears.

▼ In spring, enormous herds of caribou (reindeer) migrate north to feed on the plants of the tundra.

115 The floating ice layer over the Arctic Ocean cracks and melts around the edges to form dangerous pack ice (icebergs) and icefields. Around the shores of the Arctic Ocean, massive lumps of ice break from ice sheets and form glaciers (frozen rivers), which float out into the ocean as icebergs.

116 Around the Arctic Ocean it is too cold and windy for any trees to grow. The main plants are tussock grass, small bushes, low-growing mosses and lichens. These treeless zones are known as tundra. The Arctic hares that live here have very short ears, to stop them losing body heat.

117 Around the tundra, millions of conifers form huge areas known as boreal forests, or taiga. These are some of Earth's last unexplored wildernesses. Conifer trees' needle-like leaves and downward-sloping branches mean that snow slides off easily. If too much snow gathered, the branches would become heavy and break.

118 The deer known as caribou in North America are called reindeer in northern Europe and Asia. They wander through the forests in winter, then trek out to tundra areas for the summer, in long journeys known as migrations. Packs of wolves follow them and pick off the old, young, sick and dying.

119 In some Arctic regions, the soil just below the surface never thaws, even in summer. These areas are called permafrost. The layer of ice does not let surface water drain through down into the soil below. So permafrost areas are usually boggy and swampy.

FLOATING ICEBERG

Icebergs are much bigger than they look. Make a big lump of ice by putting a plastic bowl of water into a freezer. Float this lump in a sink filled with water. How much is above the surface? In an iceberg it is usually about one-eighth of the total volume above, leaving seven-eighths below.

▶ When there is less ice in summer, brown bears wander from the forests towards the Arctic Ocean shores.

Sea around a frozen land

120 Antarctica is different to the Arctic in many ways. The Arctic is a sea surrounded by land, while the Antarctic is land surrounded by sea. Antarctica is a huge landmass about 14 million square kilometres in area, mostly covered by ice. It has mountains, valleys, and old volcanoes, but nearly all of these are hidden under the ice.

Corrie (bowl)

Glacier

Crevasses (cracks)

Melting nose or snout

Squeezed snow and ice

▶ Snow and ice slide slowly from the polar ice caps as long glaciers, down to the sea.

121 Around Antarctica is the Southern Ocean, also called the Antarctic or Southern Polar Ocean. It is larger and deeper than the Arctic Ocean, with an area of around 20 million square kilometres and an average depth of 4500 metres. It merges into southern parts of the Atlantic, Indian and Pacific Oceans.

◀ Massive chunks split off the ice cap into the sea, and float away as they melt.

122 During the long, dark winter, the Antarctic ice sheet spreads into the surrounding ocean. It forms layers known as ice shelves, which float on the surface. As summer arrives, the shelves shrink back again.

123 Huge ice blocks break off the ice shelves to form massive icebergs. This ice was originally snow, so it is made of fresh water. It differs from the sea ice that forms in the middle of the Arctic Ocean.

124 Each summer, a small area of Antarctica becomes ice-free. This is mainly along the Antarctic Peninsula towards South America. The land is mostly rock and thin soil, where only a few small plants and animals can survive.

I DON'T BELIEVE IT!

Antarctica's ice cap is an average of 1600 metres deep. In places the ice goes down 3350 metres before reaching the rocky surface of the continent. Here there are streams, rivers and lakes, all far below the ice surface.

▶ Most of an iceberg is hidden below the sea's surface, and sometimes scrapes along the sea bed.

Animals of Arctic lands

125 Many kinds of animals live on the lands of the far north. Most of them have thick fur or feathers to keep out the cold and wind in winter. In spring, they shed (moult) their winter fur or feathers, and grow a thinner summer coat.

◄ Ptarmigan change their feathers for camouflage, from white in winter to brownish in summer.

126 Snowy owls make nests on the tundra. They lay their eggs in shallow hollows in the ground. The female looks after her chicks while the male finds food.

► Snowy owl chicks feed on small animals such as mice, voles, lemmings and young birds.

127 The ptarmigan gets new feathers for winter. In preparation for the colder months, the ptarmigan grows thick, white feathers. These help it to merge into the natural background, which is known as camouflage. Its winter feathers are also warmer than its brown summer feathers.

WHITE ON WHITE

How do snowy owls 'hide' out in the open? Make a snowy owl by cutting out an owl face shape and feathers from white paper. Draw the eyes and beak. Hold the owl in front of surfaces of different colours. See how it stands out more against dark colours and less against pale colours.

◀ The Arctic ground squirrel hibernates for up to seven months every year. When it emerges from its burrow it feeds mostly on a variety of plants, seeds and berries.

130 In North America, musk oxen live out on the tundra. They have very long, thick fur, with some hairs reaching almost one metre in length. Herds of musk oxen are hunted by arctic wolves. If the adult musk oxen sense danger, they form a defensive circle around their young to protect them.

128 Smaller animals of the far north include the Arctic hare, snowshoe hare, various kinds of voles, Siberian and Norway lemmings, and Arctic ground squirrels. Some of them live under the snow in winter, which is warmer than out in the freezing winds above.

129 The moose of North America is known as the elk in Europe. It eats all kinds of plant foods, from soft waterweeds in summer to twigs and bark in winter. Some move south in autumn to the shelter of the forests for the cold winter. Only the males have antlers.

▶ The moose, or elk, is the biggest deer. A large male can be 2 metres in height.

Realm of bears and wolves

▲ Arctic foxes often follow polar bears, to feed on the leftover bits of their kill.

131 The biggest land hunter in the Arctic, and in the world, is the polar bear. However it often hunts in water and on ice, too! A big male polar bear can measure 3 metres in length and weigh over half a tonne.

132 The polar bear's favourite food is seals. Camouflaged against the snow, polar bears hunt by creeping up on their prey, then pouncing. They also wait by seals' breathing holes for one to appear above the water. Then the bear bites the seal or hooks it out of the water with its huge claws.

▶ In midwinter, the mother polar bear gives birth to two or three tiny babies, called cubs, in a snow cave she digs.

133 Polar bears can swim for hours in icy water, and walk across land, ice or frozen snow. Their fur is very thick, and their paws are wide so they sink less in soft snow. They also have a layer of fat under their skin, called blubber, which keeps in body heat.

▼ Wolves try to break up and scatter a herd of musk oxen so they can attack the young.

134 Wolves of the far north tend to follow their prey, such as caribou and musk oxen, until it tires. Wolves work in packs to kill a large victim, or they can hunt alone for smaller prey such as Arctic hares, voles and lemmings.

135 Only the chief male and female of the wolf pack (the alpha pair), mate and have cubs. Other pack members help look after the cubs, and bring them food. They also help to defend the pack from polar bears and brown bears.

Arctic seals

136 **Many kinds of seals live in the Arctic region.** These include ringed seals, bearded seals, harp seals, spotted seals, ribbon seals and hooded seals. Most feed on fish, squid and small shrimp-like creatures called krill, which are also eaten by whales.

◄ Seals make breathing holes by bashing their noses, teeth and flippers against the thin ice.

137 **Seals have very thick fur to keep out the cold water.** Like their main enemy, the polar bear, they also have a layer of fatty blubber under the skin to keep them warm. They swim well but have to come up to breathe every few minutes. Sometimes they use breathing holes they make in the ice.

138 **In spring, mother seals come onto the ice to give birth.** Their babies, or pups, have very thick, fluffy fur to keep them warm. Each mother seal usually has only one pup. She feeds it on very rich milk, and it grows very quickly.

▼ Walruses often use their flippers and tusks to haul themselves out of the water onto rocky shores, to sunbathe during the brief summer.

139 **Mother seals have to return to the water to feed, leaving their pups alone on the ice.** At this time pups are in danger from polar bears, wolves and other predators. Within a couple of weeks the young seal is big enough to look after itself.

140 **The walrus is a huge seal with two long upper teeth, called tusks.** It shows these off at breeding time to impress its partner. Tusks are also used in feeding, to lever shellfish off the seabed. A big walrus can grow to 3 metres in length and weigh 1.5 tonnes!

Whales of the far north

142 The beluga is also called the white whale. It makes a variety of sounds such as whistles, squeals, twitters and chirps. These can be heard even above the surface. Old-time sailors nicknamed it the 'sea canary'. Both the beluga and narwhal are 4 to 6 metres in length and weigh about one tonne. They eat prey such as fish, squid and shellfish.

▲ The beluga whale has very bendy lips, and purses them as though kissing, to suck in its food.

143 The beluga and narwhal migrate within the Arctic, from the southern areas of the Arctic Ocean to the even icier waters further north. They follow the edge of the ice sheet as it shrinks each spring, then grows back again each autumn.

141 The cold seas of the Arctic are visited in summer by many kinds of whales, including the biggest of all, the blue whale. However, there are some whales that stay in the Arctic all year round, such as the beluga and narwhal.

I DON'T BELIEVE IT!
The massive bowhead whale has the largest head and mouth of any animal. Its head is almost one-third of its 18 metre-long-body. The brush-like baleen strips in its huge curved mouth can be more than 4 metres in length!

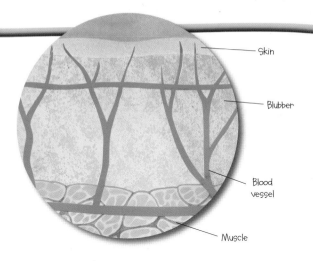

Skin

Blubber

Blood vessel

Muscle

▲ Whales, seals and other polar mammals have a thick layer of blubber under their skin. In whales it is about five times thicker than the fat beneath human skin.

145 The northern right and the bowhead whale are baleen whales. They have long brush-like fringes of baleen in their mouths to filter tiny animals, called plankton, from the sea. These whales can weigh up to 80 tonnes! They are among the world's rarest whales, with just a few hundred right whales left.

144 The male narwhal has a tooth in its upper jaw that grows very long and pointed, to form a spear-like tusk. This can reach 3 metres in length. It is sometimes used to pierce a hole in the ice so the whale can come up to breathe.

146 One of the most powerful Arctic hunters is the killer whale, or orca. It is not a true whale, but the largest kind of dolphin. It lives in large family groups called pods and hunts fish, seals and even great whales.

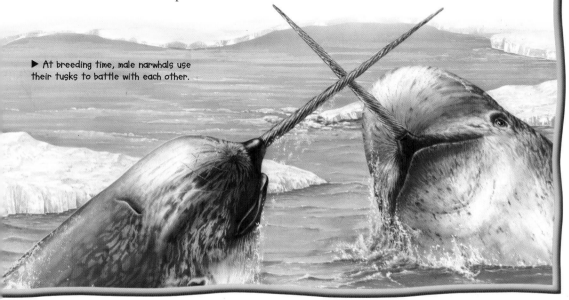

▶ At breeding time, male narwhals use their tusks to battle with each other.

Summer visitors

147 **Some animals migrate north to the Arctic for its short summer.** At this time, Arctic days are long and food is plentiful. In autumn, as the long winter approaches, animals return south to warmer regions.

148 **The Arctic tern has the longest migration of all animals.** It breeds in summer at the Arctic, then follows the warm weather south to the Antarctic, to have another summer. It covers an amazing 35,000 kilometres every year.

▼ The Arctic tern swoops down to the sea's surface to eat small creatures such as baby fish and krill.

▼ Snow geese flock to the tundra of North America in huge family groups, where each pair raises three to five chicks.

149 The mighty sperm whale is also a summer visitor to the Arctic. The huge males swim from the tropics to the edge of the pack ice. They dive to great depths to catch fish and giant squid.

▲ Grey whale babies (calves) join their mothers on the long journey north each spring, but many are attacked by sharks and killer whales.

150 Many kinds of geese and other birds migrate to the Arctic in summer, such as snow geese, Brent geese and barnacle geese. These birds make nests and rear their chicks quickly. They feed on grasses, rushes, sedges and other plants of the boggy tundra, as well as eating flies, grubs and other small creatures from pools along the seashore.

151 Grey whales swim along the coasts of the North Atlantic in spring, to feed in the waters off Alaska and in the Bering Sea throughout the summer. Then they return to subtropical waters off Baja California, Mexico, and spend the winter resting and giving birth. Their yearly journeys total 20,000 kilometres, and are the longest migration of any mammal.

QUIZ

Do some research and see if you can put these animals in order of the distance they cover on their yearly migration:

A Bowhead whale
B Barnacle goose
C Sperm whale
D Arctic tern
E Caribou

Answers:
D C B E A

In the Southern Ocean

152 During summer, the Southern Ocean around Antarctica is rich with life. The water is not very warm, but it contains many nutrients and there is lots of daylight. This means billions of tiny plants and animals, called plankton, grow. They become food for bigger creatures such as fish and squid.

153 The great supply of krill and plankton attracts some huge visitors to the Antarctic region. These include the world's largest animals, such as the blue whale, fin whale and humpback whale, which migrate here for summer.

154 Southern Ocean seals include the leopard, crabeater and Southern elephant seal. Despite its name, the crabeater seal does not actually eat crabs – it is mainly a krill-feeder. The leopard seal is about 3 metres in length and very fierce. It catches fish, seabirds, penguins, and even other seals.

155 A Southern elephant seal is almost as big as a real elephant! These seals spend weeks at sea feeding, then come to remote beaches to breed. The huge males, called beachmasters, rear up, roaring and biting each other, before mating with the females.

▼ Male elephant seals battle each other to win an area of the beach, otherwise they do not breed. Sometimes they become badly injured in the fight, and die.

156 Elephant seals are the deepest-diving of all seals. They can dive down more than 1000 metres and stay under the water for over an hour before they need to surface for breath. They eat mainly fish and squid, as well as crabs and shrimps from the ocean floor.

I DON'T BELIEVE IT!

A male southern elephant seal can be more than 5 metres in length. When it is well fed, it weighs almost two tonnes! It gets its name from its huge size, and from its long, floppy nose.

71

Antarctic waters

157 Apart from seals, whales, fish and squid, many other creatures thrive in Antarctic waters. They include jellyfish that drift with the currents, trailing their long tentacles. The tentacles sting passing creatures, which are then pulled up to the mouth on the underside of the jellyfish's umbrella-like body (bell).

158 The temperature of polar seas often falls below 0°C. However, the waters do not always freeze, so animals are safe from being frozen solid. This is because sea water contains salts, so its freezing point is lower than fresh water. Ice crystals also break up as they form, due to the movement of the seas' currents and waves.

▼ The *Isotealia* anemone lives in waters from about 50 to 500 metres deep. It grabs any kind of food, including jellyfish and sea urchins.

► The huge desmonema jellyfish grows to more than one metre across. It catches fish, krill, sea worms and starfish.

159 Cousins of jellyfish, known as sea anemones, also live along the coasts of Antarctic islands. They too have stinging tentacles that pull in prey such as shrimps and prawns. However the mainland shores of Antarctica itself are too cold for most kinds of seaside animals.

QUIZ

Do some research to find out which fish is most closely related to the Antarctic ice-fish.

A Flatfish
B Sharks
C Trout
D Perch

Answer: D

160 Several polar fish have special substances in their blood and body fluids that work like natural anti-freeze. Even if trapped in solid ice, these animals can survive for a while by going into suspended animation – staying still and using almost no energy.

▶ There are several kinds of Antarctic ice-fish, which have blood that is thickened by certain natural chemicals to stop it freezing.

73

Antarctic birds

161 Antarctica is visited by hundreds of kinds of birds each year. Most of them fly over the open ocean, since there is very little unfrozen land on which to nest. In contrast, the islands close to Antarctica are home to some breeding birds, such as albatrosses and petrels.

162 The wandering albatross has longer wings than any other bird, at more than 3 metres from tip to tip. Albatrosses form long-lasting breeding pairs that come together on remote islands to raise their single chick. The young albatross may not fly until it is almost one year old.

▼ Research scientists measure the wingspan of an albatross.

▶ Tussock birds are always on the lookout for any morsels of food. This bird is pecking bits of flaking skin from an elephant seal.

163 The blackish cinclodes, also called the tussock bird, eats almost anything it can find. It snaps up shellfish and shrimps along the coast and eats dead crabs and starfish washed up on the shore. Tussock birds also wander around seabird colonies to feed on the rotting fish that the parent birds cough up, or regurgitate, for their chicks.

164 Skuas are powerful seabirds with large, sharp beaks. They chase terns, gulls and similar birds and attack them in mid air, forcing them to drop their food, which the skua then gulps down.

▶ The skua's strong beak can easily stab into a penguin's egg. Then the bird laps up the soft inner parts or hacks apart the chick inside.

Sliding and diving

165 Penguins live only in the south, around Antarctica — there are none in the Arctic. They cannot fly, but they use their flipper-like wings to swim with great speed and skill. Most of the 17 kinds of penguins live on the islands and shores of the Southern Ocean, on the icebergs and ice floes there, and on the continent of Antarctica itself.

▼ Penguins' outer feathers overlap in water or when the weather is cold, and stand upright when it is warmer.

Long feathers

Down feathers

Skin

1. Long feathers overlap, trapping warm air next to the skin

Warm air escaping

Long feathers

Down feathers

Skin

2. Long feathers separate, letting warm air escape

166 The biggest penguins are emperors. They can be up to 120 centimetres in height and weigh more than 30 kilograms. They breed on Antarctic ice, and the female lays just one egg, passes it over to the male, and leaves. She sets off on the long journey back to the sea to feed.

▶ Adelie penguins slide down an icy cliff and take to the water, in search of their main food — krill.

STAND UP!

You will need:
card   felt-tip pens   tape

Make a penguin about 30 centimetres tall from card. Carefully cut out the head and body, two flippers, and two feet, and colour them with felt-tip pens. Tape the parts together and try to make the penguin stand upright. It's quite tricky! Luckily a penguin has a short, stiff tail. Cut this out and tape it on to make standing easier.

167 The male emperor penguin spends almost two months of the worst midwinter weather with the egg on his feet, keeping it warm until it hatches. Then the female returns, walking and sliding across the ice, to take over caring for the chick. At last the hungry male can head to the sea to feed.

168 The king penguin is the second-largest penguin. It stands about 90 centimetres in height and weighs up to 15 kilograms. Its main foods are fish, squid and plankton. King penguins can dive down to 200 metres.

▲ Emperor penguins travel to traditional breeding sites to find a partner and mate. When an egg hatches, the parent bird brings up (regurgitates) food from its stomach to feed its chick.

Polar peoples

169 People have lived in Arctic regions for over 10,000 years. Today, groups exist around northern North America, Scandinavia (northern Europe) and Siberia (north Asia). They include Inuit, Aleuts, Koryak, and Chukchi people. They live in some of the world's most difficult conditions.

I DON'T BELIEVE IT!

Wind chill makes cold temperatures much worse! Cold wind blowing past a warmer object, such as a human body, draws away heat in seconds. If the temperature is −20°C, strong winds can double this to −40°C. It freezes body parts in seconds.

170 In recent times, the traditional way of life in polar regions has changed greatly. New ways of travel are available, from skidoos and other snowmobiles to helicopters, snowplanes and icebreaker ships. Many polar people are no longer cut off from the lands farther south. They can trade more easily for consumer goods such as clothes, tools, TVs and prepared foods.

▼ Snowmobiles have skis at the front for steering, and tracks at the rear to push the vehicle along. Here, a Saami person crosses a snow-covered lake in Finland.

171 Commercial fishing is big business in some Arctic areas. Ships catch large numbers of fish or krill, especially in summer. Whaling and sealing are banned, but ships continue to catch food that these animals eat, so the populations can still be harmed.

▶ Traditional fishing skills are still vital. This man is fishing for halibut through a hole in the ice in Greenland.

172 One of the most helpful modern items for northern people has been the gun. In the past, spears or hooks and lines were used to catch seals and other food. Even when using guns, hunters still need patience. Arctic animals are very wary and it is difficult to creep up on them unseen in the white, icy wilderness.

▼ Tourism is a growing business in Ilulissat, Greenland, a World Heritage Site. Visitors come to see icebergs breaking off the Sermeq Kujalleq glacier.

173 The discovery of oil, coal, minerals and other resources have brought many newcomers to the Arctic. Settlements have grown up along the coasts. The houses are heated by oil, from wells in the area, or coal mined locally, since there are no trees to burn as fuel.

Living in the cold

174 Over time, Arctic people have developed skills and knowledge to survive in this harsh environment. Plants are scarce, so food is mainly animals such as seals, shellfish, fish and whales. A stranded whale can provide enough food for a week.

1. Large blocks of squashed snow or loose ice are cut with a large-bladed snow-knife.

2. The blocks are stacked in a circular pattern, sloping inwards in a gradually rising spiral.

3. The blocks slope together to make a dome shape that keeps out wind and snow.

175 Arctic animals provide not just food, but many other resources for polar people. The fatty blubber is burned in lamps for heat and warmth. Weatherproof clothes and boots are made from the furry skins of seals, caribou and other creatures.

176 Tools and utensils such as knives, bowls and spoons are also made from local animals. They are carved from the bones and teeth of smaller toothed whales, from the horns of caribou and musk oxen, from the tusks of walrus and narwhals, and from the bendy, springy baleen or whalebone of great whales.

◀ Snow houses called igloos are usually a temporary shelter, made for just a night or two while out on a winter hunting expedition.

▶ Kayaks are usually paddled by hand with paddles made from driftwood. Some modern ones have outboard motors. Here, a kayak is launched by hunters in Alaska.

177 Since so much food is obtained from the sea, boats are very useful. The canoe-like kayak is made by stretching waterproof animal skin such as whale hide over a frame of carved driftwood, or perhaps bone. The parts are tied together with animal sinews.

178 Kayaks are light and easily carried, and slide well across snow and ice. Larger kayaks are used for carrying a family's possessions to a new hunting area.

◀ The joints between the blocks in an igloo are sealed with snow to keep out the wind. The entrance is low down to prevent the warm air inside from escaping.

QUIZ

Try and find out which materials Antarctic people use to make the following items:

A. Boots
B. An overcoat
C. A head-dress

Answers:
A. Waterproof sealskin
B. Reindeer hide
C. Seabird feathers

81

Life of a herder

179 Some people of the far north live inland. People in northern Europe such as the Saami (Lapps), and the Nenet of Siberia, depend on reindeer herds that provide them with almost everything they need.

▼ Nenet people gather reindeer in a herd to be checked and counted.

180 The reindeer herds follow their natural migrations. They move north to tundra areas for summer and head south to the forests for winter. Herders travel with them, to keep the herds together and protect them from wolves and bears.

181 As the people and deer move, the reindeer pull sleds loaded with the herder's tents, utensils and other belongings. The animals are counted regularly and spare reindeer are herded to the local towns, where they are traded for items such as sharp metal knives.

I DON'T BELIEVE IT!

In the last 50 years the Nenet people have lost more than 7 million hectares of reindeer grazing lands due to pollution, the creation of coal mines, new vehicle tracks, oil pipelines, and introduced animals eating the plant food.

182 Reindeer can provide a huge variety of resources.

Their fur and skins make clothes, boots, floor rugs, sleeping blankets and tents. They provide fresh milk and blood to drink, and their meat is very nutritious. The antlers and bones are carved into utensils and tools. They are also used, along with teeth, to make beautiful works of art, showing scenes of fishing, hunting, herding and the natural world.

▲ Saami hunters live in tents of reindeer hide stretched over log poles, which can be easily packed and transported by sled.

On top of the world!

183 **Many adventurers have tried to reach the North Pole, which is located near the middle of a floating layer of ice in the Arctic Ocean.** Before today's satellite navigation, it was hard to know if you were in the right place. Then, explorers had to prove that they really did reach their destination. They couldn't leave a flag in the floating, breaking ice.

▶ Nansen's ship *Fram* was stuck in ice for almost three years, but its design meant that it survived.

184 **English admiral William Parry tried to reach the North Pole in 1825.** So did Norwegian explorer Fridtjof Nansen in 1893–96 in his ship *Fram*. Yet neither of them made it. In 1909, American Robert Peary and his team claimed to have reached the North Pole, but experts do not agree if they really did.

185 **The first people to fly over the North Pole in a plane may have been Richard Byrd and Floyd Bennet in 1926.** However, as with Peary, it's not certain if they really did. A few days later, Roald Amundsen – the first person to reach the South Pole – flew over the North Pole in an airship, the *Norge*.

◀ Some experts disagree with Robert Peary's claim that he marched across the floating ice to the North Pole.

186 Claims to be first to stand at the North Pole continued, such as Russian explorer Pavel Gordiyenko and his team in 1952. In 1968, American explorer Ralph Plaisted and two colleagues made the first surface trip there.

187 In modern times, more and more expeditions have reached the North Pole across the ice. In 2007, Dutch performer Guido van der Werve spent a day there, turning in the opposite direction to the Earth's spinning, so in fact he stayed completely still. It is even possible for rich tourists to fly to the exact North Pole for a few hours' visit.

▼ In 2007, Lewis Gordon Pugh swam one kilometre through water in cracks between the North Pole ice, to highlight the problem of global warming.

Race to the South Pole

189 Once ships arrived at Antarctica, there was still a dangerous journey across the ice to the South Pole. Irish explorer Ernest Shackleton made several trips there. In 1901–02 in the ship *Discovery*, and in 1914–16 in *Endurance*. These trips did not reach the South Pole, but helped to establish bases for further exploring across the ice cap.

▶ In Ernest Shackelton's 1914–15 expedition, his ship *Endurance* was frozen into the ice for ten months and finally crushed. Yet all the crew were eventually rescued.

188 It was difficult to even get close to the South Pole. In 1820, Russian naval officer Fabian Gottlieb von Bellingshausen was perhaps the first person to see the Antarctic mainland. American seal-hunter John Davis may have been first to set foot on the continent, in 1821. In 1839, English naval commander James Clark Ross set sail on a voyage to map Antarctica's outline. Many of these people have areas of Antarctica named after them.

SLIPPERY SLOPE

You will need:
length of wood   ice cubes   stones   wood   plastic

Hold up one end of the wood, like a ramp. Put an ice cube at the top and let it slide down. The ice melts into water, which works like slippery oil. Try sliding the other substances such as plastic, wood and stone. The ramp has to be much steeper!

▲ Amundsen's expedition saved the weight of carrying food by killing and eating the sled dogs one by one.

190

In 1911 two expeditions set off to reach the South Pole, led by Norwegian Roald Amundsen, and English naval officer Robert Scott. The world was gripped by news of their 'race to the Pole'. Amundsen, his team and his dog sleds got there first on 14 December 1911, and returned safely. Scott and his team, pulling their own sledges, arrived a month later. Tragically, on the way back they ran out of supplies and were stranded by blizzards. They did not survive.

191

The South Pole can now be visited by rich tourists. Several overland expeditions make the trek each year. There is a permanent scientific base called the Amundsen-Scott South Pole Station, where people live and work, usually for a period of six months.

▶ In 1997, mother-of-two Laurence de la Ferriere walked across Antarctica to the South Pole unaided.

Polar lands in peril

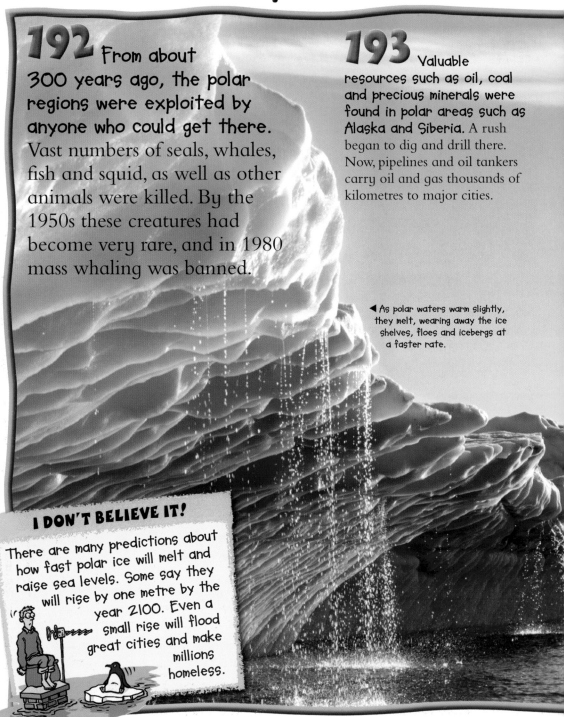

192 From about 300 years ago, the polar regions were exploited by anyone who could get there. Vast numbers of seals, whales, fish and squid, as well as other animals were killed. By the 1950s these creatures had become very rare, and in 1980 mass whaling was banned.

193 Valuable resources such as oil, coal and precious minerals were found in polar areas such as Alaska and Siberia. A rush began to dig and drill there. Now, pipelines and oil tankers carry oil and gas thousands of kilometres to major cities.

◀ As polar waters warm slightly, they melt, wearing away the ice shelves, floes and icebergs at a faster rate.

I DON'T BELIEVE IT!

There are many predictions about how fast polar ice will melt and raise sea levels. Some say they will rise by one metre by the year 2100. Even a small rise will flood great cities and make millions homeless.

194
Pollution has begun to affect the polar lands. Dangerous chemicals such as pesticides from farming, and toxins from industry, flow into Arctic waters. The protective ozone layer above Antarctica has been made thinner by chemicals from aerosol spray cans. Oil spills from tankers have devastated parts of the Arctic.

195
Climate change will have terrifying results around the world. The habitats of polar bears, seals, penguins and many other animals are disappearing. Floods will affect low-lying areas far from polar lands, where billions of people live in cities. Polar scientific bases have been set up to study these problems.

▼ The striped pole marks the exact spot of the South Pole. It is repositioned every New Year's Day, as the ice moves around 10 metres yearly.

▶ Cleaning penguins' coats of pollution strips their feathers of natural oils, without which the birds could freeze to death. Rescued birds are fitted with woolly jumpers to keep them warm.

196
The greatest threat to polar regions may still be to come. Global warming due to the greenhouse effect is causing climate change, as world temperatures rise. This is making the ice caps melt, causing sea levels to rise.

Protecting the Poles

197 Countries have signed agreements to protect polar lands and oceans from damage. Even tourism can be a problem. Cruise ships bring visitors that disturb whales and other wildlife, and leave waste.

▼ Scientists monitor emperor penguin breeding colonies near the Weddell Sea, Antarctica, to see the effect of climate change on their breeding.

198 In 1994 the Southern Ocean was declared a vast sanctuary, or safe area, for whales. This meant it was also safe for many other kinds of wildlife. However some countries still hunt whales, and ships also go there to catch krill, fish and squid. As we catch more, whales and other large animals have less to eat.

199 Some parts of the Arctic are also being protected. Some countries want to drill for oil and gas, and mine for coal, precious minerals and metals. Big companies sometimes try to change the minds of governments or break the rules. These activities create jobs for people, but create risks of pollution.

QUIZ

Arrange these ways of travelling across polar lands from fastest to slowest:

A. Walk
B. Skidoo
C. Ski
D. Dog-pulled sled

Answer:
Fastest to slowest – D C B A

200 The polar lands and oceans are far away from most of us. Yet they are the last great wildernesses on Earth. They have the harshest habitats in the world, where animals have had to adapt or perish. These places need our help to survive.

91

Water world

201 Oceans cover more than two–thirds of the Earth's rocky surface. Their total area is about 362 million square kilometres, which means there is more than twice as much ocean as land! Although all the oceans flow into each other, we know them as four different oceans – the Pacific, Atlantic, Indian and Arctic. Our landmasses, the continents, rise out of the oceans.

ARCTIC OCEAN

ATLANTIC OCEAN

PACIFIC OCEAN

ATLANTIC OCEAN

SOUTHE..

202 The largest, deepest ocean is the Pacific. It covers nearly half of our planet and is almost as big as the other three oceans put together! In places, the Pacific is so deep that the Earth's tallest mountain, Everest, would sink without a trace.

The deepest parts of the Pacific would cover Mount Everest without trace

▶ Mount Everest is the highest point on Earth, rising to 8848 metres. Parts of the Pacific Ocean are deeper than 10,000 metres.

Light hits the surface of the water

Scattered blue and green

▶ A cup of sea water appears see-through. It is only when you look at a large area of sea that it has colour.

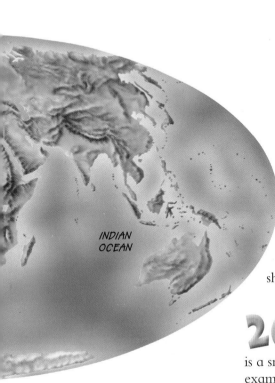

INDIAN OCEAN

▲ The world's oceans cover most of our planet. Each ocean is made up of smaller bodies of water called seas.

203 **Oceans can look blue, green or grey.** This is because of the way light hits the surface. Water soaks up the red parts of light but scatters the blue-green parts, making the sea look different shades of blue or green.

204 **Seas can be red or dead.** A sea is a small part of an ocean. The Red Sea, for example, is the part of the Indian Ocean between Egypt and Saudi Arabia. Asia's Dead Sea isn't a true sea, but a landlocked lake. We call it a sea because it is a large body of water.

205 **There are streams in the oceans.** All the water in the oceans is constantly moving, but in some places it flows as currents, which take particular paths. One of these is the warm Gulf Stream, that travels around the edge of the Atlantic Ocean.

I DON'T BELIEVE IT!
Oceans hold 97 percent of the world's water. Just a fraction is in freshwater lakes and rivers.

Ocean features

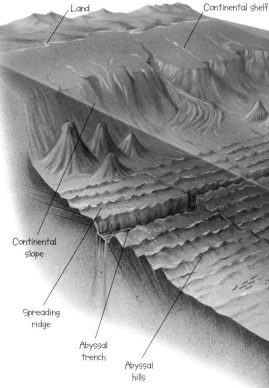

Land Continental shelf

Continental slope

Spreading ridge

Abyssal trench

Abyssal hills

▲ Under the oceans there is a landscape similar to that found on land.

206 There are plains, mountains and valleys under the oceans, in areas called basins. Each basin has a rim (the flat continental shelf that meets the shore) and sides (the continental slope that drops away from the shelf). In the ocean basin there are flat abyssal plains, steep hills, huge underwater volcanoes called seamounts, and deep valleys called trenches.

▼ Magma (molten rock) escapes from the seabed to form a ridge. This ridge has collapsed to form a rift valley.

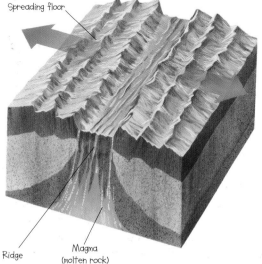

Spreading floor

Ridge Magma (molten rock)

207 The ocean floor is spreading. Molten (liquid) rock inside the Earth seeps from holes on the seabed. As the rock cools, it forms new sections of floor that creep slowly out. Scientists have proved this fact by looking at layers of rock on the ocean floor. There are matching stripes of rock either side of a ridge. Each pair came from the same hot rock eruption, then slowly spread out.

Sea mount

Volcanic island

Ocean trench

▼ An atoll is a ring–shaped coral reef that encloses a deep lagoon. It can form when a volcanic island sinks underwater.

1. Coral starts to grow

4. Coral atoll is left behind

2. Lagoon appears around volcano

3. Volcano disappears

208 Some islands are swallowed by the ocean.

Sometimes, a ring-shaped coral reef called an atoll marks where an island once was. The coral reef built up around the island. After the volcano blew its top, the reef remained.

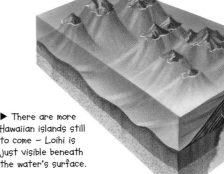

▶ There are more Hawaiian islands still to come – Loihi is just visible beneath the water's surface.

209 New islands are born all the time.

When an underwater volcano erupts, its lava cools in the water. Layers of lava build up, and the volcano grows in size. Eventually, it is tall enough to peep above the waves. The Hawaiian islands rose from the sea like this.

I DON'T BELIEVE IT!

The world's longest mountain chain is under the ocean. It is the Mid-Ocean range and stretches around the middle of the Earth.

Tides and shores

210 **The sea level rises and falls twice each day along the coast.** This is known as high and low tides. Tides happen because of the pull of the Moon, which lifts water from the part of the Earth's surface facing it.

▼ At high tide, the sea rises up the shore and dumps seaweed, shells and drift wood. Most coasts have two high tides and two low tides every day.

High tides happen at the same time each day on opposite sides of the Earth

At high tide the water level rises

At low tide the water level goes down again

211 **Spring tides are especially high.** They occur twice a month, when the Moon is in line with the Earth and the Sun. Then, the Sun's pulling force joins the Moon's and seawater is lifted higher than usual. The opposite happens when the Moon and Sun are at right angles to the Earth. Then, their pulling powers work against each other causing weak neap tides – the lowest high tides and low tides.

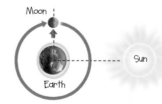

◄ Neap tides occur when the Sun and Moon are at right angles to each other and pulling in different directions.

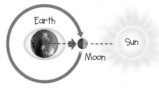

► Spring tides occur when the Sun and the Moon are lined up and pulling together.

212 The sea is strong enough to carve into rock. Pounding waves batter coastlines and erode, or wear away, the rock.

▶ Waves can create amazing shapes such as pillars called sea stacks.

Sea stack

Arch

▲ A tsunami can travel faster than a jumbo jet.

215 Tidal waves are the most powerful waves. Also known as tsunamis, they happen when underwater earthquakes trigger tremendous shock waves. These whip up a wall of water that travels across the sea's surface.

213 Sand is found on bars and spits, as well as beaches. It is made up of grains of worn-down rock and shell. Sand collects on shorelines and spits, but also forms on offshore beaches called sand bars. Spits are narrow ridges of worn sand and pebbles.

214 Some shores are swampy. This makes the border between land and sea hard to pinpoint. Muddy coastlines include tropical mangrove swamps that are flooded by salty water from the sea.

▶ The stilt-like roots of mangrove trees take in both air and water.

I DON'T BELIEVE IT!

The biggest tsunami was taller than five Statues of Liberty! It hit the Japanese Ryuku Islands in 1771.

Life in a rock pool

216 **Rock pools are teeming with all kinds of creatures.** Limpets are a kind of shellfish. They live on rocks and in pools at shorelines. Here, they eat slimy, green algae, but they have to withstand the crashing tide. They cling to the rock with their muscular foot, only moving when the tide is out.

217 **Some anemones fight with harpoons.** Beadlet anemones will sometimes fight over a feeding ground. Their weapon is the poison they usually use to stun their prey. They shoot tiny hooks like harpoons at each other until the weakest one gives in.

▲ Anemones are named after flowers, because of their petal-like arms.

218 **Starfish can grow new arms.** They may have as many as 40 arms, or rays. If a predator grabs hold of one, the starfish abandons the ray, and uses the others to make its getaway!

◄ Starfish are relatives of brittle stars, sea urchins and sea cucumbers.

219 Hermit crabs do not have shells. Most crabs shed their shells as they outgrow them, but the hermit crab does not have a shell. It borrows the leftover shell of a dead whelk or other mollusc – whatever it can squeeze into to protect its soft body. These crabs have even been spotted using a coconut shell as a home!

▶ Hermit crabs protect their soft bodies in a borrowed shell.

FIND THE SHELL

Can you find the names of four shells in the puzzle below ?

**1. alcm   2. lesmus
3. teroys 4. hewkl**

Answers:
1. Clam 2. Mussel
3. Oyster 4. Whelk

220 Sea urchins wear a disguise. Green sea urchins sometimes drape themselves with bits of shell, pebble and seaweed. This makes the urchin more difficult for predators, or hunters, to spot.

◀ There are about 4500 different types of sponge in the sea.

221 Sponges are animals! They are very simple creatures that filter food from sea water. The natural sponge that you might use in the bath is a long-dead, dried-out sponge.

Colourful coral

222 **Tiny animals build huge underwater walls.** These are built up from coral, the leftover skeletons of sea creatures called polyps. Over millions of years, enough skeletons pile up to form huge, wall-like structures called reefs. Coral reefs are full of hidey-holes and make brilliant habitats for all sorts of amazing, colourful sea life.

223 **The world's biggest shellfish lives on coral reefs.** Giant clams grow to well over one metre long – big enough for you to bathe in its shell!

224 **Seahorse dads have the babies.** They don't exactly give birth, but they store the eggs in a pouch on their belly. When the eggs are ready to hatch, a stream of miniature seahorses billows out from the dad's pouch.

▶ Baby seahorses stream out of their father's pouch and into the sea.

Parrot fish

Giant clam

Clownfish

225 Some fish go to the cleaners.

Cleaner wrasse are little fish that are paid for cleaning! Larger fish, such as groupers and moray eels visit the wrasse, which nibble all the parasites and other bits of dirt off the bigger fishes' bodies – what a feast!

226 Clownfish are sting-proof. Most

creatures steer clear of an anemone's stinging tentacles. But the clownfish swims among the stingers, where it's safe from predators. Strangely, the anemone doesn't seem to sting the clownfish.

I DON'T BELIEVE IT!

You can see the Great Barrier Reef from space! At over 2000 km long, it is the largest structure ever built by living creatures.

Lion fish

Cleaner wrasse fish

227 Some fish

look like stones. Stone fish rest on the seabed, looking just like the rocks that surround them. If they are spotted, the poisonous spines on their backs can stun an attacker in seconds.

Stone fish

▲ Tropical coral reefs are the habitat of an amazing range of marine plants and creatures.

Swimming machines

228 There are over 21,000 different types of fish in the sea. They range from huge whale sharks to tiny gobies. Almost all are covered in scales and use fins and a muscular tail to power through the water. Like their freshwater cousins, sea fish have slits called gills that take oxygen from the water so they can breathe.

229 The oarfish is bigger than an oar – it is as long as four canoes! It is the longest bony fish and is found in all the world's oceans. Oarfish are handsome creatures – they have a striking red fin along the length of their back.

◄ People once thought oarfish swam horizontally through the water. Now they know they swim upright.

▶ At over 3 metres long, sunfish are the biggest bony fish in the oceans. They feed on plankton.

230 Sunfish like sunbathing! Ocean sunfish are very large, broad fish that can weigh as much as a tonne. They are named after their habit of sunbathing on the surface of the open ocean.

▶ Flying fish feed near the surface so they are easy to find. Their gliding flight helps them escape most hunters.

232

Flying fish cannot really fly. Fish can't survive out of water, but flying fish sometimes leap above the waves when they are travelling at high speeds. They use their wing-like fins to keep them in the air for as long as 30 seconds.

QUIZ

1. Which fish like to sunbathe?
2. How many types of fish live in the sea?
3. How does a fish breathe?
4. Can flying fish really fly?

Answers:
1. Sunfish 2. 21,000 3. With its gills 4. No

▲ In a large group called a school, fish like these yellow snappers have less chance of being picked off by a predator.

231 Not all fish are the same

shape. Cod or mackerel are what we think of as a normal fish shape, but fish come in all shapes and sizes. Flounder and other flatfish have squashed-flat bodies. Eels are so long and thin that the biggest types look like snakes, while tiny garden eels resemble worms! And of course, seahorses and seadragons look nothing like other fish at all!

▶ The flounder's flattened shape and dull colouring help to camouflage (hide) it on the seabed.

Shark!

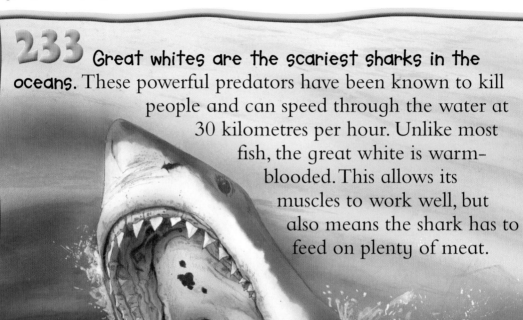

233 Great whites are the scariest sharks in the oceans. These powerful predators have been known to kill people and can speed through the water at 30 kilometres per hour. Unlike most fish, the great white is warm-blooded. This allows its muscles to work well, but also means the shark has to feed on plenty of meat.

▼ Basking sharks eat enormous amounts of plankton. They sieve through around 1000 tonnes of water every hour.

▲ Great white sharks are fierce hunters. They will attack and eat almost anything, but prefer to feed on seals.

234 Most sharks are meat-eaters. Herring are a favourite food for sand tiger and thresher sharks, while a hungry tiger shark will gobble up just about anything! Strangely, some of the biggest sharks take the smallest prey. Whale sharks and basking sharks eat tiny sea creatures called plankton.

SHARK PARTS

Study the labels to learn the shark's special features. Trace the shark without the labels, then see how many parts you can name.

▶ Hammerheads prey on other sharks and rays, bony fish, crabs and lobsters, octopus and squid.

Dorsal fin

Ampullae of Lorenzini (to sense electricity from nearby fish)

Gill

Nostril

Jaw

Pectoral fin

Pelvic fin

Anal fin

Tail fin

236 Hammerhead sharks have a hammer-shaped head! With a nostril and an eye on each end of the 'hammer', they swing their head from side to side. This gives them double the chance to see and sniff out any signs of a tasty catch.

▼ Tiger sharks leave their newborn pups to fend for themselves.

235 Tiger sharks may have as many as 40 pups! The baby sharks develop in eggcases inside their mother's body. Many other sharks also reproduce like this, but it is not the only way. Hammerhead and grey reef shark babies develop inside their mother, not in eggcases. Other sharks, such as dogfish and zebra sharks, lay eggcases straight into the sea, leaving the babies to fend for themselves.

Whales and dolphins

237 The biggest animal on the planet lives in the oceans. It is the blue whale, measuring about 28 metres in length and weighing up to 190 tonnes. It feeds by filtering tiny, shrimp-like creatures called krill from the water – about four tonnes of krill a day! Like other great whales, it has special, sieve-like parts in its mouth called baleen plates.

▲ As the sperm whale surfaces, it pushes out stale air through its blowhole. It fills its lungs with fresh air and dives down again.

238 Whales and dolphins have to come to the surface for air. This is because they are mammals, like we are. Sperm whales hold their breath the longest. They have been known to stay underwater for nearly two hours.

▶ Blue whale calves feed on their mother's rich milk until they are around eight months old.

▲ Killer whales carry the baby seals out to sea before eating them.

► The beluga is a type of white whale. It makes a range of noises – whistles, clangs, chirps and moos!

241 Killer whales play with their food.
They especially like to catch baby seals, which they toss into the air before eating. Killer whales are not true whales, but the largest dolphins. They have teeth for chewing, instead of baleen plates.

239 Dolphins and whales sing songs to communicate.
The noisiest is the humpback whale, whose wailing noises can be heard for hundreds of kilometres. The sweetest is the beluga – nicknamed the 'sea canary'. Songs are used to attract a mate, or just to keep track of each other.

242 Moby Dick was a famous white whale.
It starred in a book by Herman Melville about a white sperm whale and a whaler called Captain Ahab.

240 The narwhal has a horn like a unicorn's.
This Arctic whale has a long, twirly tooth that spirals out of its head. The males use their tusks as a weapon when they are fighting over females.

I DON'T BELIEVE IT!
Barnacles are shellfish. They attach themselves to ships' hulls, or the bodies of grey whales and other large sea animals.

▲ The narwhal's 3 metre tusk seems too long for its body.

Sleek swimmers

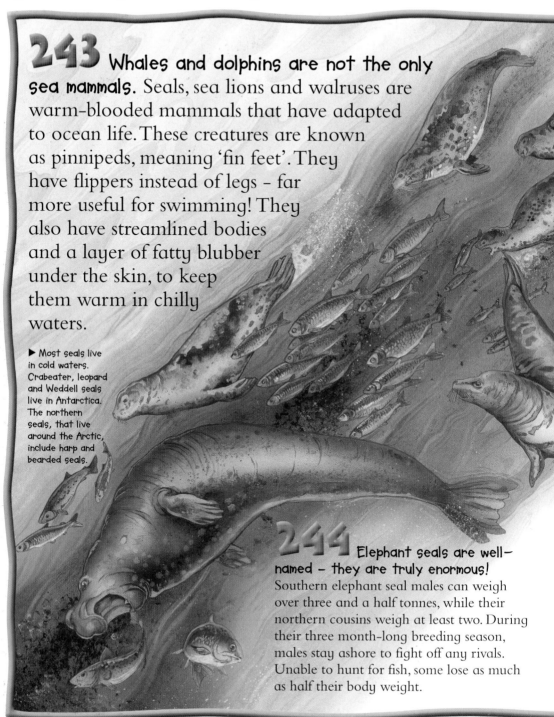

243 **Whales and dolphins are not the only sea mammals.** Seals, sea lions and walruses are warm-blooded mammals that have adapted to ocean life. These creatures are known as pinnipeds, meaning 'fin feet'. They have flippers instead of legs – far more useful for swimming! They also have streamlined bodies and a layer of fatty blubber under the skin, to keep them warm in chilly waters.

▶ Most seals live in cold waters. Crabeater, leopard and Weddell seals live in Antarctica. The northern seals, that live around the Arctic, include harp and bearded seals.

244 **Elephant seals are well-named – they are truly enormous!** Southern elephant seal males can weigh over three and a half tonnes, while their northern cousins weigh at least two. During their three month-long breeding season, males stay ashore to fight off any rivals. Unable to hunt for fish, some lose as much as half their body weight.

246 Sea otters anchor themselves when they sleep. These playful creatures live off the Pacific coast among huge forests of giant seaweed called kelp. When they take a snooze, they wrap a strand of kelp around their body to stop them being washed out to sea.

▲ Anchored to the kelp, a sea otter is free to crack open a crab shell – and snack!

245 Walruses seem to change colour! When a walrus is in the water, it appears pale brown or even white. This is because blood drains from the skin's surface to stop the body losing heat. On land, the blood returns to the skin and walruses can look reddish brown or pink!

▼ Walruses use their tusks as weapons. They are also used to break breathing holes in the ice, and to help the walrus pull itself out of the water.

I DON'T BELIEVE IT!

Leopard seals sing in their sleep! These seals, found in the Antarctic, chirp and whistle while they snooze.

109

Ocean reptiles

247 Marine iguanas are the most seaworthy lizards. Most lizards prefer life on land, where it is easier to warm up their cold-blooded bodies, but marine iguanas depend on the sea for their food. They dive underwater to graze on the algae and seaweed growing on rocks.

▲ Marine iguanas are found around the Galapagos Islands in the Pacific. When they are not diving for food, they bask on the rocks that dot the island coastlines. The lizards' dark skin helps to absorb the Sun's heat.

248 Turtles come ashore only to lay their eggs. Although they are born on land, turtles head for the sea the minute they hatch. Females return to the beach where they were born to dig their nest. After they have laid their eggs, they go straight back to the water. Hawksbill turtles may lay up to 140 eggs in a clutch, while some green turtle females clock up 800 eggs in a year!

▲ In a single breeding season, a female green turtle may lay as many as ten clutches, each containing up to 80 eggs!

249

There are venomous (poisonous) snakes in the sea. Most stay close to land and come ashore to lay their eggs. Banded sea snakes, for example, cruise around coral reefs in search of their favourite food, eels. But the yellow-bellied sea snake never leaves the water. It gives birth to live babies in the open ocean.

▼ Banded sea snakes use venom (poison) to stun prey, but the yellow-bellied sea snake has a sneakier trick. Once its colourful underside has attracted some fish, it darts back – so the fish are next to its open mouth! The venom of sea snakes is more powerful than that of any land snake.

Banded sea snake

Yellow-bellied sea snake

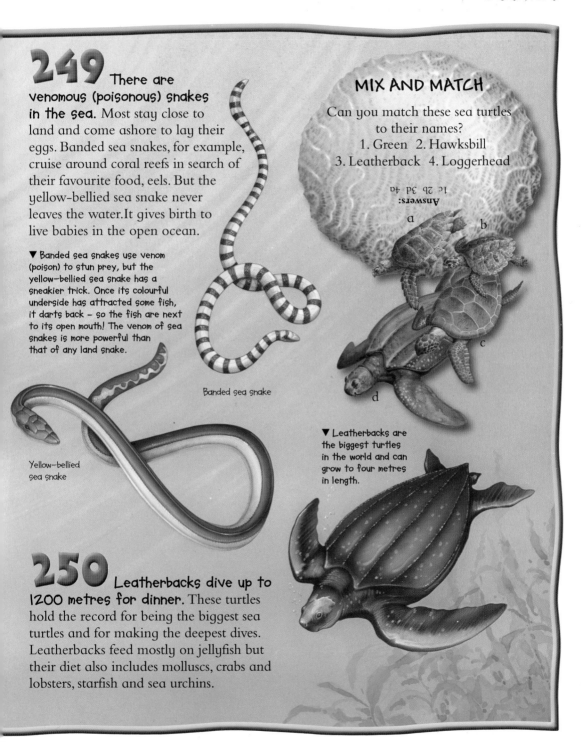

MIX AND MATCH

Can you match these sea turtles to their names?
1. Green 2. Hawksbill
3. Leatherback 4. Loggerhead

Answers:
1c 2b 3d 4a

a

b

c

d

▼ Leatherbacks are the biggest turtles in the world and can grow to four metres in length.

250

Leatherbacks dive up to 1200 metres for dinner. These turtles hold the record for being the biggest sea turtles and for making the deepest dives. Leatherbacks feed mostly on jellyfish but their diet also includes molluscs, crabs and lobsters, starfish and sea urchins.

Icy depths

251 Few creatures can survive in the dark, icy-cold ocean depths. Food is so hard to come by, the deep-sea anglerfish does not waste energy chasing prey – it has developed a clever fishing trick. A stringy 'fishing rod' with a glowing tip extends from its dorsal fin or hangs above its jaw. This attracts smaller fish to the anglerfish's big mouth.

▼ Anglerfish are black or brown for camouflage. Only their glowing 'fishing rod' is visible in the gloom.

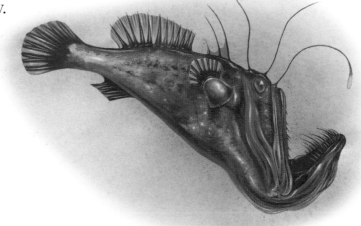

▼ The light created by deep-sea fish, or by bacteria living on their bodies, is known as biological light, or bioluminescence.

Lantern fish

Cookiecutter shark

Dragon fish

252 Some deep-sea fish glow in the dark. As well as tempting prey, light also confuses predators. About 1500 different deep-sea fish give off light. The lantern fish's whole body glows, while the dragon fish has light organs dotted along its sides and belly. Just the belly of the cookiecutter shark gives off a ghostly glow. Cookiecutters take biscuit-shaped bites out of their prey's body!

253
Black swallowers are greedy-guts! These strange fish are just 25 centimetres long but can eat fish far bigger than themselves. Their loose jaws unhinge to fit over the prey. Then the stretchy body expands to take in their enormous meal.

▶ The viperfish is named for its long, snake-like fangs.

▼ Like many deep-sea fish, black swallowers have smooth, scaleless skin.

254
Viperfish have teeth which are invisible in the dark. They swim around with their jaws wide open. Deep-sea shrimp often see nothing until they are right inside the viperfish's mouth.

▼ Tubeworms grow around deep-sea volcanoes called black smokers.

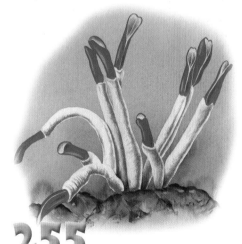

I DON'T BELIEVE IT!

Female deep-sea anglerfish grow to 120 centimetres in length, but the males are a tiny six centimetres!

255
On the seabed, there are worms as long as cars! These are giant tubeworms and they cluster around hot spots on the ocean floor. They feed on tiny particles that they filter from the water.

Amazing journeys

256 Many ocean animals travel incredible distances. Spiny lobsters spend the summer feeding off the coast of Florida, but head south in autumn to deeper waters. They travel about 50 kilometres along the seabed, in columns that may be more than 50-strong. They keep together by touch, using their long, spiky antennae (feelers).

▲ In spring, spiny lobsters return to shallower waters. They spawn (lay their eggs) around the coral reefs off the Straits of Florida.

257 Arctic terns are the long-distance flying champs. These seabirds fly farther than any other bird. After nesting in the Arctic, they head south for the Antarctic. In its lifetime, one bird might cover more than 1,250,000 kilometres!

◄ In a single year, an Arctic tern may fly more than 40,000 kilometres!

258

Grey whales migrate, or travel, farther than any other mammal. There are two main grey whale populations in the Pacific. One spends summer off the Alaskan coast. In winter they migrate south to Mexico to breed. The whales may swim nearly 20,000 kilometres in a year. The other grey whale group spends summer off the coast of Russia, then travels south to Korea.

▶ Grey whales spend summer in the Bering Sea, feeding on tiny, shrimp-like creatures called amphipods. They spend their breeding season, December to March, in the warmer waters off Mexico.

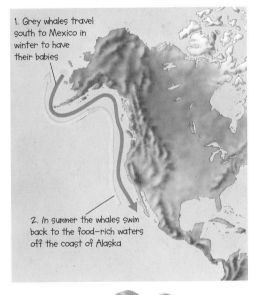

1. Grey whales travel south to Mexico in winter to have their babies

2. In summer the whales swim back to the food-rich waters off the coast of Alaska

259

Baby loggerhead turtles make a two-year journey. They are born on beaches in Japan. The hatchlings hurry down to the sea and set off across the Pacific to Mexico, a journey of 10,000 kilometres. They spend about five years there before returning to Japan to breed.

▼ Not all loggerhead hatchlings make it to the sea. As they race down the beach, some are picked off by hungry gulls or crabs.

I DON'T BELIEVE IT!

Eels and salmon swim thousands of kilometres from the sea to spawn in the same river nurseries where they were born.

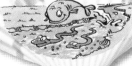

On the wing

Albatross

260 **Wandering albatrosses are the biggest sea birds.** An albatross has a wingspan of around three metres – about the length of a family car! These sea birds are so large, they take off by launching from a cliff. Albatrosses spend months at sea. They are such expert gliders that they even sleep on the wing. To feed, they land on the sea, where they sit and catch creatures such as squid.

◀ A gannet dives and captures a fishy meal in its beak.

261 **Gannets wear air–bag shock absorbers.** The gannet's feeding technique is to plummet headfirst into the ocean and catch a fish in its beak. It dives at high-speed and hits the water hard. Luckily, the gannet's head is protected with sacs of air that absorb most of the shock.

262 Puffins nest in burrows.

While many birds jostle for space on a high cliff ledge, puffins dig a burrow on the clifftop. Here, they lay a single egg. Both parents feed the chick for the first six weeks.

▼ Puffins often scrape their own burrows, or they may take over an abandoned rabbit hole.

263 Boobies dance to attract a mate.

There are two types of booby, blue or red-footed. The dancing draws attention to the male's colourful feet. Perhaps this stops the females from mating with the wrong type of bird.

▼ Boobies are tropical seabirds that nest in colonies.

264 Frigate birds puff up a balloon for their mate.

Male frigate birds have a bright-red pouch on their throat. They inflate, or blow up, the pouch as part of their display to attract a female.

▲ A frigate bird shows off to its mate.

117

Perfect penguins

265 Macaroni, Chinstrap, Jackass and Emperor are all types of penguin. There are 17 different types in total, and most live around the Antarctic. Penguins feed on fish, squid and krill. Their black-and-white plumage is important camouflage. Seen from above, a penguin's black back blends in with the water. The white belly is hard to distinguish from the sunlit surface of the sea.

Chinstrap penguin

266 Penguins can swim, but not fly. They have oily, waterproofed feathers and flipper-like wings. Instead of lightweight, hollow bones – like a flying bird's – some penguins have solid, heavy bones. This enables them to stay underwater longer when diving for food. Emperor penguins can stay under for 15 minutes or more.

I DON'T BELIEVE IT!

The fastest swimming bird is the Gentoo penguin. It has been known to swim at speeds of 27 kilometres per hour!

▶ Penguins have a layer of fat under their feathers to protect them in the icy water.

Gentoo penguin

Adélie penguin

King penguin

Emperor penguin

267 Emperor penguin dads balance an egg on their feet.

They do this to keep their egg off the Antarctic ice, where it would freeze. The female leaves her mate with the egg for the whole two months that it takes to hatch. The male has to go without food during this time. When the chick hatches, the mother returns and both parents help to raise it.

▶ A downy Emperor penguin chick cannot find its own food in the sea. It must wait until it has grown its waterproof, adult plumage.

▲ An Adélie penguin builds its nest from stones and small rocks.

268 Some penguins build stone circles.

This is the way that Adélie and Gentoo penguins build nests on the shingled shores where they breed. First, they scrape out a small dip with their flippered feet and then they surround the hollow with a circle of pebbles.

Harvests from the sea

◀ Fishermen attach buoys to their lobster pots, so they can remember where to find them again.

269 **Oysters come from beds – and lobsters from pots!** The animals in the oceans feed other sea creatures, and they feed us, too! To gather oysters, fishermen raise them on trays or poles in the water. First, they collect oyster larvae, or babies. They attract them by putting out sticks hung with shells. Lobster larvae are too difficult to collect, but the adults are caught in pots filled with fish bait.

270 **Some farmers grow seaweed.** Seaweed is delicious to eat, and is also a useful ingredient in products such as ice cream and plant fertilizer. In shallow, tropical waters, people grow their own on plots of seabed.

▲ The harvested seaweed can be dried in the sun to preserve it.

▶ The oil platform's welded-steel legs rest on the seabed. They support the platform around 15 metres above the surface of the water.

Derrick

Crane

Helicopter landing pad

Flare

Oil processing area

271 Sea minerals are big business.

Minerals are useful substances that we mine from the ground – and oceans are full of them! The most valuable are oil and gas, which are pumped from the seabed and piped ashore or transported in huge supertankers. Salt is another important mineral. In hot, low-lying areas, people build walls to hold shallow pools of sea water. The water dries up in the sun, leaving behind crystals of salt.

272 There are gemstones under the sea.

Pearls are made by oysters. If a grain of sand is lodged inside an oyster's shell, it irritates its soft body. The oyster coats the sand with a substance called nacre, which is also used to line the inside of the shell. Over the years, more nacre builds up and the pearl gets bigger.

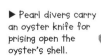

QUIZ

1. What are the young of lobster called?
2. What substances are pumped from the seabed?
3. Is seaweed edible?
4. Which gemstone is made by oysters?

Answers:
1. Larvae 2. Oil and gas
3. Yes 4. Pearl

▶ Pearl divers carry an oyster knife for prising open the oyster's shell.

First voyages

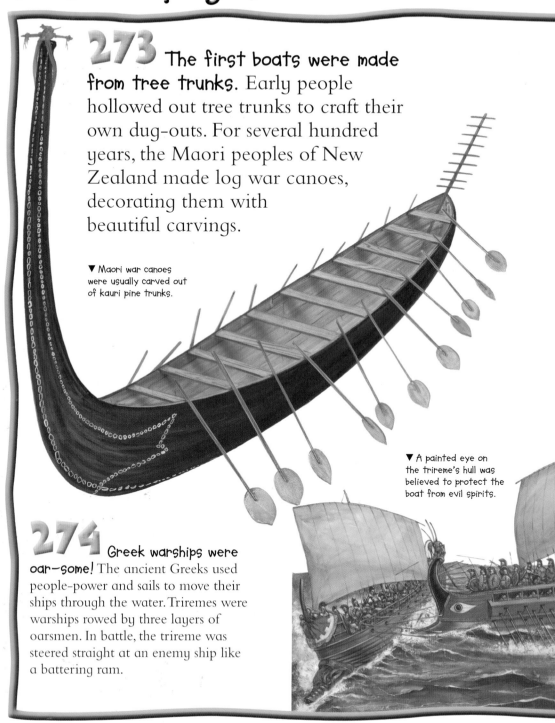

273 **The first boats were made from tree trunks.** Early people hollowed out tree trunks to craft their own dug-outs. For several hundred years, the Maori peoples of New Zealand made log war canoes, decorating them with beautiful carvings.

▼ Maori war canoes were usually carved out of kauri pine trunks.

▼ A painted eye on the trireme's hull was believed to protect the boat from evil spirits.

274 **Greek warships were oar-some!** The ancient Greeks used people-power and sails to move their ships through the water. Triremes were warships rowed by three layers of oarsmen. In battle, the trireme was steered straight at an enemy ship like a battering ram.

▼ Viking longboats were clinker–built, which means that they were made of overlapping planks of wood.

277 **Boats found the way to a new world.** The 1400s were an amazing time of exploration and discovery. One explorer, Christopher Columbus, set sail from Spain in 1492 with a fleet of three ships. He hoped to find a new trade route to India, but instead he found the Americas! Before then, they were not even on the map!

▶ Columbus's fleet consisted of the *Niña*, the *Pinta* and the *Santa Maria.*

275 **Dragons guarded Viking longboats.** Scandinavian seafarers decorated their boats' prows with carvings of dragons and serpents to terrify their enemies. Built from overlapping planks, Viking longboats were very seaworthy. Leif Ericson was the first Viking to cross the Atlantic Ocean to Newfoundland, in North America just over 1000 years ago.

276 **It is thought that Chinese navigators made the first compass–like device about 2500 years ago.** Compasses use the Earth's magnetism to show the directions of north, south, east and west. They are used at sea, where there are no landmarks. The navigators used lodestone, a naturally magnetic rock, to magnetize the needle.

▶ Early compasses were very simple. During the 1300s compasses became more detailed.

BOAT SCRAMBLE!

Unscramble the letters to find the names of six different types of boat.

1. leacvar 2. chenroos
3. rarlewt 4. coclear
5. leglay 6. pecpril

Answers:
1. Caravel 2. Schooner
3. Trawler 4. Coracle
5. Galley 6. Clipper

Pirates!

278 **Pirates once ruled the high seas.** Pirates are sailors who attack and board other ships to steal their cargoes. Their golden age was during the 1600s and 1700s. This was when heavily laden ships carried treasures, weapons and goods back to Europe from colonies in the Americas, Africa and Asia. Edward Teach, better known as Blackbeard, was one of the most terrifying pirates. He attacked ships off the coast of North America during the early 1700s. To frighten his victims, it is said that he used to set fire to his own beard!

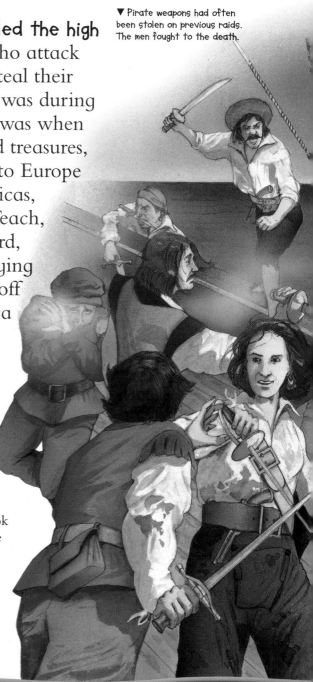

▼ Pirate weapons had often been stolen on previous raids. The men fought to the death.

279 **There were women pirates, too.** Piracy was a man's world, but some women also took to the high seas. Mary Read and Anne Bonny were part of a pirate crew sailing around the Caribbean. They wore men's clothes and used fighting weapons, including daggers, cutlasses and pistols.

280 There are still pirates on the oceans.

Despite police patrols who watch for pirates and smugglers, a few pirates still operate. Luxury yachts are an easy target and in the South China Sea, pirate gangs on motor boats even attack large merchant ships.

▼ Divers have found some extraordinary hoards of treasure on board sunken galleons.

281 There is treasure lying under the sea.

Over the centuries, many ships sunk in storms or hit reefs. They include pirate ships loaded with stolen booty. Some ships were deliberately sunk by pirates. The bed of the Caribbean Sea is littered with the remains of Spanish galleons, many of which still hold treasure!

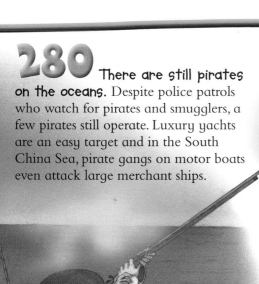

PIRATE FLAG!

You will need:

paper   paints   brushes

The skull-and-crossbones is the most famous pirate flag, but it was not the only one. Copy one of these designs!

Going under

282 A submarine has dived deeper than 10,000 metres.
The two-person *Trieste* made history in 1960 in an expedition to the Mariana Trench in the Pacific, the deepest part of any ocean. It took the submarine five hours to reach the bottom, a distance of 10,911 metres. On the way down, the extreme water pressure cracked part of the craft, but luckily, the two men inside returned to the surface unharmed.

▲ *Trieste* spent 20 minutes at the bottom of the Mariana Trench. The trench is so deep, you could stack the CN Tower inside it 19 times (left)!

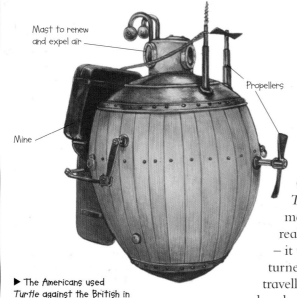

Mast to renew and expel air

Propellers

Mine

▶ The Americans used *Turtle* against the British in their War of Independence.

283 The first combat submarine was shaped like an egg!
Turtle was a one-person submarine that made its test dive in 1776. It was the first real submarine. It did not have an engine – it was driven by a propeller that was turned by hand! *Turtle* was built for war. It travelled just below the surface and could fix bombs to the bottom of enemy ships.

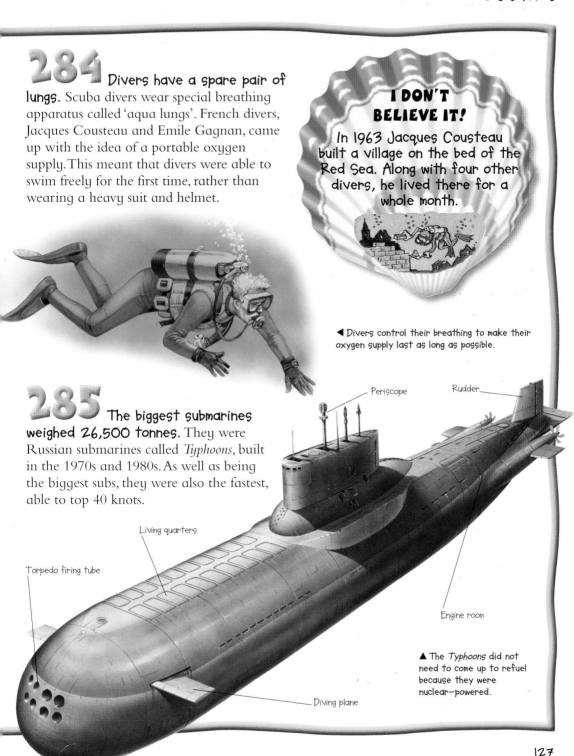

284
Divers have a spare pair of lungs. Scuba divers wear special breathing apparatus called 'aqua lungs'. French divers, Jacques Cousteau and Emile Gagnan, came up with the idea of a portable oxygen supply. This meant that divers were able to swim freely for the first time, rather than wearing a heavy suit and helmet.

I DON'T BELIEVE IT!
In 1963 Jacques Cousteau built a village on the bed of the Red Sea. Along with four other divers, he lived there for a whole month.

◀ Divers control their breathing to make their oxygen supply last as long as possible.

285
The biggest submarines weighed 26,500 tonnes. They were Russian submarines called *Typhoons*, built in the 1970s and 1980s. As well as being the biggest subs, they were also the fastest, able to top 40 knots.

Periscope

Rudder

Living quarters

Torpedo firing tube

Engine room

Diving plane

▲ The *Typhoons* did not need to come up to refuel because they were nuclear-powered.

Superboats

286 Some ships are invisible.
Stealth warships are not really
invisible, of course, but they are
hard to detect using radar.
There are already materials
being used for ships that can
absorb some radar signals.
Some paints can soak up radar,
too, and signals are also bounced
off in confusing directions by the
ships' strange, angled hulls.

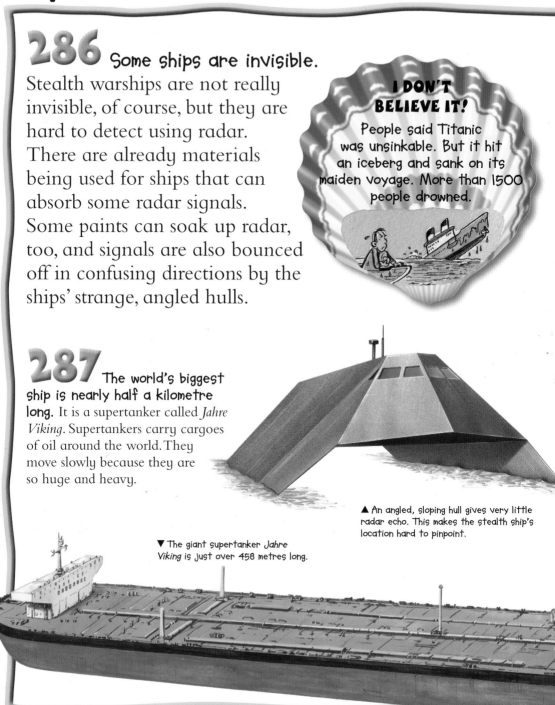

287 The world's biggest
ship is nearly half a kilometre
long. It is a supertanker called *Jahre
Viking*. Supertankers carry cargoes
of oil around the world. They
move slowly because they are
so huge and heavy.

▲ An angled, sloping hull gives very little
radar echo. This makes the stealth ship's
location hard to pinpoint.

▼ The giant supertanker *Jahre
Viking* is just over 458 metres long.

288 Not all boats ride the waves. Hovercrafts sit slightly above the water. They have a rubbery skirt that traps a cushion of air for them to ride on. Without the drag of the water to work against, hovercraft can cross the water much faster.

◄ Hovercraft can travel at up to 65 knots, the equivalent of 120 kilometres per hour.

▼ *Freedom Ship* will be over 1300 metres long. Aircraft 'taxis' will be able to take off and land on its rooftop runway.

289 Ships can give piggy-backs! Heavy-lift ships can sink part of their deck underwater, so a smaller ship can sail aboard for a free ride. Some ships carry planes. Aircraft carriers transport planes that are too small to carry enough fuel for long distances. The deck doubles up as a runway, where the planes take off and land.

290 *Freedom Ship* will resemble a floating city. It will be one of the first ocean cities, with apartments, shopping centres, a school and a hospital. The people who live on *Freedom* will circle the Earth once every two years. By following the Sun, they will live in constant summertime!

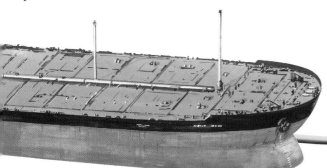

Riding the waves

291 **The first sea sport was surfing.** It took off in the 1950s, but was invented centuries earlier in Hawaii. Hawaii is still one of the best places to surf – at Waimea Bay, surfers catch waves that are up to 11 metres high. The record for the longest rides, though, are made off the coast of Mexico, where it is possible to surf for more than 1.5 kilometres.

▶ Modern surfboards are made of super–light materials. This means they create little drag in the water – and the surfer can reach high speeds!

292 **A single boat towed 100 waterskiers!** This record was made off the coast of Australia in 1986 and no one has beaten it yet. The drag boat was a cruiser called *Reef Cat*.

◀ Water skiing is now one of the most popular of all water sports.

QUIZ

1. What was the name of the fastest hydroplane?
2. When did jetskis go on sale?
3. Where is Waimea Bay?
4. What is a trimaran?

Answers:
1. Spirit of Australia
2. 1973 3. Hawaii
4. A three-hulled boat

293 Jetskiers can travel at nearly 100 kilometres per hour.

Jetskis were developed in the 1960s. Their inventor was an American called Clayton Jacobsen who wanted to combine his two favourite hobbies, motorbikes and waterskiing. Today, some jetskiers are professional sportspeople.

◄ Jetskis first went on sale in 1973.

▼ Trimarans have three hulls, while catamarans have two.

294 Three hulls are sometimes better than one.

Powerboating is an exciting, dangerous sport. Competitors are always trying out new boat designs that will race even faster. Multi-hulled boats minimize drag, but keep the boat steady. Trimarans have three slender, streamlined hulls that cut through the water.

► Hydroplanes are motor boats that skim across the surface of the water.

295 Hydroplanes fly over the waves.

They are a cross between a boat and a plane. Special 'wings' raise the hull two metres above the water. The fastest hydroplane ever was *Spirit of Australia*. Driven by Kenneth Warby, it sped along at more than 500 kilometres per hour above the surface of the water!

Ocean stories

▼ Jason and the Argonauts steer their ship between two huge moving cliffs called the Cyanean Rocks. They faced many dangers on their journey.

296 **The Greek hero Jason made an epic sea voyage.** The ancient Greeks made up lots of sea adventure stories, probably because they lived on scattered islands. In the legend of the Argonauts, a hero called Jason sets off in a boat called the *Argos* with a band of brave men. He goes on a quest to find the Golden Fleece, a precious sheepskin guarded by a fierce dragon.

297 **Neptune (or Poseidon) was an undersea god.** Poseidon was the name used by the ancient Greeks and Neptune by the ancient Romans. Both civilizations pictured their god with a fork called a trident. They blamed their gods for the terrible storms that wrecked boats in the Mediterranean.

▶ Neptune raises his trident and whips up a storm.

▲ The beautiful goddess Aphrodite emerges from the sea.

299 Long ago, people believed in a giant sea monster, called the kraken. The stories were used to explain the dangers of the sea. Sightings of the giant squid might have inspired these tales.

▶ Mistaken for a monster! The 15 metre-long giant squid has eyes as big as dinner plates.

298 The Greek goddess of love was born in the sea.

Aphrodite, said to be the daughter of Zeus, was born out of the foam of the sea. The Romans based their love goddess, Venus, on the same story. Lots of artists have painted her rising from the waves in a giant clam shell.

300 Mermaids lured sailors to their deaths on the rocks. Mythical mermaids were said to be half-woman, half-fish. Folklore tells how the mermaids confused sailors with their beautiful singing – with the result that their ships were wrecked on the rocks.

▼ Mermaids were said to have a fishy tail instead of legs.

I DON'T BELIEVE IT!

A mermaid's purse is the name given to the eggcases of the dog shark. They look a little bit like handbags!

133

Wonders of the world

301 **In the world's rainforests animals and plants are closely linked in a daily struggle for survival.** It's a battle for life that has been going on for millions of years, and has led to these unique environments becoming home to a huge variety of living things, from the deadliest frogs to the foulest-smelling flowers.

▼ In a rainforest, plants of all types fight for light and space. They create an emerald-green landscape of leafy undergrowth and towering trees.

What is a rainforest?

302 Rainforests are places where lots of rain falls every year – usually more than 2000 millimetres. They are filled with enormous, broad-leaved trees and a bewildering collection of living things. Rainforests usually grow in warm, steamy parts of the world.

303 Trees provide habitats (homes) for millions of rainforest animals and plants. Much of the wildlife in these forests cannot survive anywhere else – just one of the reasons why people want to make sure rainforests are kept safe.

Toco toucan

304 Of all the different habitats found on Earth, rainforests have the biggest range of living things. They are home to more than 80 percent of all insects and a single rainforest in South America has 18,000 different types of plants. The word 'biodiversity' is used to describe the range of living things that live in one habitat.

Tapir

EMERGENT LAYER

CANOPY

UNDERSTOREY

FOREST FLOOR

Queen Alexandra's
birdwing butterfly

305 Rainforests have four main layers. The bottom layers are the dark, dank forest floor and understorey, where the shortest plants live. Here, bugs, frogs, fungi and many other living things thrive. The middle layer is the forest canopy and the top layer is the emergent layer. This is where the tallest trees poke up above a blanket of green leaves. The trees are home to vines, mosses, monkeys, lizards, snakes, insects and thousands of species (types) of bird.

◄ Most animals and plants live in the rainforest canopy layer. The understorey is very gloomy because not much sunlight reaches it.

I DON'T BELIEVE IT!

People who live in rainforests can build their entire homes from plant materials. Walls are made from palm stems or bamboo and leaves can be woven to make roofs and floors.

Red-eyed
tree frog

306 Rainforests are home to people as well as animals and plants. Many tribes (groups of people) live in these dense, green forests around the world, finding food, medicines and shelter amongst the trees. Some of them still follow a traditional lifestyle, hunting animals and gathering plants for food.

Not just jungles

307 Hot, steamy rainforests are sometimes called jungles. They are found in Earth's tropical regions. These are areas near the Equator, an imaginary line that encircles the Earth, where daily temperatures are around 25°C and it rains most days.

▼ A boy rows a canoe made from a hollow tree trunk on the Amazon River in Brazil.

308 Around 60–100 million years ago, most of the world's land was covered with tropical rainforest. Now only a tiny area – six percent – is covered. This is partly due to deforestation (people cutting down trees) and partly because the Earth's climate has changed, becoming cooler and drier.

309 Temperate rainforests grow in cool, wet places. 'Temperate' means having a moderate climate. Trees here are usually conifers such as pine trees. Temperate rainforests are home to the world's largest trees – Californian redwoods. These can live for 2000 years, and the tallest reach 115 metres in height.

▶ Redwoods, or sequoias, are giant trees that sprout from tiny seeds. The trees produce cones that each contain up to 300 seeds.

▶ Mangrove trees grow long and tangled roots, which slow down the movement of water and create a habitat for animals.

310
Mangrove swamps are another type of warm, wet rainforest.
The trees that grow here live with their roots steeped in layers of mud, silt and salty water. Around half of the world's mangrove forests have been cut down in the last 50 years and it is expected that almost all mangrove forests will have disappeared by 2050.

311
Rainforests on mountains higher than 2500 metres are often shrouded in mist. They are given the name 'cloud forests', and here the temperatures are lower than in a tropical rainforest. Mosses, ferns and liverworts are plants that thrive in these permanently damp conditions. The trunk and branches of a tree in a cloud forest can be completely covered in a bright-green coating of moss.

▶ Cloud forests can be eerie places where trees and plants are permanently shrouded in a fine mist.

HUG A TREE!
Visit a local woodland or forest and find out the names of some of its trees. Use a sketchbook or camera to record images of wildlife you see there. Find out which are the widest tree trunks by hugging them. Can you find one that is so broad your fingers don't touch?

Where in the world?

312 Tropical forests grow in the region close to the Equator. The area just south of the Equator is called the Tropic of Capricorn, and the area just north of the Equator is called the Tropic of Cancer.

NORTH AMERICA

▼ Grizzly bears live in forests near the Pacific coast and hunt salmon in the cold, fresh rivers.

Equator

SOUTH AMERICA

314 Amazonia is the huge tropical rainforest of Brazil and neighbouring South American countries. Further south, temperate rainforests grow, cloaked in cold mist. In the Chilean temperate rainforests, ancient trees called alerces grow. The oldest alerce is thought to have lived for over 4000 years.

313 Wet winds and cool fogs from the Pacific Ocean sweep onto the coast of North America, creating the perfect climate for temperate rainforests. This is ideal for giant conifers – evergreen trees that live there. The forests are home to black bears, mountain lions and blacktail deer.

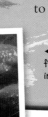

◀ Piranhas are sharp-toothed Amazon fish. They feed on a variety of animals including other fish and snails.

▲ Atlas moths are the world's largest moths. They flutter through the canopies of Asian cloud forests.

EUROPE

ASIA

▼ Cassowaries are large birds that cannot fly. They live in the forests of Australia and New Guinea.

AFRICA

◀ African bush vipers live in the forest canopy, slithering down to hunt frogs and lizards.

OCEANIA

315 Cloud forests usually grow on, or near, mountain ranges, where there is plenty of rain and mist. In China, the Yunnan cloud forest grows over tall mountains and deep gorges. The name *Yunnan* means 'south of the clouds' — it's a mysterious place that few people have visited.

Quiz

1. What is the Equator?
2. Where does the cassowary live?
3. How old is the oldest-known alerce?

Answers:
1. An imaginary line that encircles the Earth 2. New Guinea and Australia 3. More than 4000 years old

KEY 🌴 Tropical forest   🌴 Cloud forest   🌲 Temperate forest

Tree of life

316 The brazil-nut tree produces balls of seeds. Each ball is the size of a melon and as hard as stone. This amazing tree grows in tropical rainforests and provides a home and food for many living things.

317 When the seed balls are ripe they crash to the ground. Only the agouti, a dog-sized rodent, has teeth tough enough to break through the case to reach the tasty brazil nuts inside. Agoutis bury some of the nuts, which may then grow into trees. Without agoutis new brazil-nut trees could not grow.

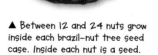

▲ Between 12 and 24 nuts grow inside each brazil-nut tree seed case. Inside each nut is a seed.

Strangler fig

318 Strangler figs grow up and around the trunks of rainforest trees. Over years, the fig continues to grow until it eventually strangles its host tree to death. Once the tree has rotted, only the tangled web of fig roots and stems remain, like a spooky tree skeleton.

◄ Agoutis' teeth continue to grow throughout their lives, allowing them to bite through nutshells.

▼ Brazil-nut tree flowers open before sunrise. By the end of the day, all the petals will have fallen off.

319 Brazil-nut trees also depend on a single type of insect to survive — orchid bees. These are the only insects strong enough to get inside the tree's heavy, hooded flowers to pollinate them, so the nuts — which contain seeds — can grow into new plants.

▶ Female orchid bees visit brazil-nut flowers to feed on nectar, while male orchid bees visit orchids to collect perfume.

320 Fallen leaves at the base of tropical trees quickly disappear. Dead matter, called leaf litter, is broken down by fungi, or eaten by bugs. This process is known as decomposition, and it helps the goodness from the leaves return to the forest soil in a natural method of recycling.

Male orchid bee

321 When a number of different living things all depend on one another for survival they are described as an ecosystem. Rainforest habitats are large ecosystems, and a brazil-nut tree is a small ecosystem. When brazil-nut trees are cut down, many other living things that depend on them die, too.

◀ A brazil-nut tree can grow to 60 metres in height and produce more than 100 kilograms of nuts every year.

143

Amazing Amazon

322 **The Amazon rainforest is the largest tropical rainforest in the world.** It covers 6 million square kilometres, which means it is nearly the same size as Australia. Around half of all animal and plant species live in Amazonia, as this forest is known.

◀ An Amazonian Hercules beetle can grow to 18 centimetres in length. It is one of the world's largest insects.

324 **Insect experts who travelled to Amazonia in the 1840s discovered more than 8000 new species (types) of beetle.** Alfred Wallace and Henry Bates were amongst the first of many scientists who realized that this rainforest has a fantastic range of animal and plant life, many of which do not exist anywhere else. Charles Darwin, a 19th century scientist, described it as 'a great wild, untidy, luxuriant hothouse'.

323 **The giant Amazon River wends its way through the forest, bringing life and death to many of its inhabitants.** This is the world's biggest river, stretching for about 6400 kilometres and pouring 770 billion litres of water into the Atlantic Ocean every day. People and animals of the forest use the river for transport, food and water.

▼ The Amazon River basin holds 20 percent of the world's fresh water.

325 The waters of the Amazon are home to many types of animal and plant. Giant waterlilies with 2-metre-wide leaves grow in slow-moving stretches of the river, but just beneath them lurk hungry alligators, sharp-toothed piranha fish and blood-sucking leeches.

326 There are more than 400 species of reptile, such as snakes and lizards, in the Amazon rainforest. More freshwater fish live in the Amazon River than anywhere else on Earth, and more than 225 types of amphibian, such as frogs and toads, live in and around the water.

▶ Large green iguanas like to lie on branches that hang over the Amazon River and soak up the sun's warming rays.

I DON'T BELIEVE IT!

Giant Amazonian leeches are blood-sucking worms that can grow up to 30 centimetres in length! They have sharp teeth and pain-numbing spit that stops blood from clotting so they can enjoy a long feast.

People of the Amazon

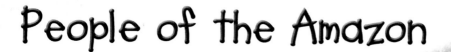

327 The Amazon was given its name by a Spanish explorer who ventured down the river in the 1540s. Francisco de Orellana was attacked by the local long-haired people who reminded him of the mythical female warriors described by the ancient Greeks, so he named the Amazon after them.

▶ Inside the *shabono*, Yanomani people build circular huts called *malocas*. At night, the young people sleep in hammocks, outside the *malacos*.

328 When Europeans first went to the Amazon rainforest in search of treasure, there were around seven million people living there. Today, 500 years later, there are fewer than a million. The Amazonian people live as groups, or tribes, and have different cultures and languages from one another.

329 The Yanomani people still follow many of their ancient traditions today. Villagers share one large home, known as the *shabono*, and women grow crops such as sweet potatoes. Men hunt using blowpipes and bows and arrows. The rainforest is the children's school, where they learn how to survive in, and protect, their jungle home.

◀ Several families make up one Yanomani village. They live, work and play together, passing on traditions and skills.

330 The Embera people use the poison produced by rainforest frogs to hunt animals to eat. Men wipe the tips of their blowpipe darts on the frogs' backs before firing them. One golden poison dart frog has enough poison to kill ten men. In recent years several rainforest frogs have become extinct (died out), but no one knows why this is.

▲ The golden poison frog produces poison on its skin, which the people of the Embera tribe carefully wipe on their darts.

331 Although many Amazonian people live in protected areas of rainforest, many more face an uncertain future. Large parts of Amazonia are being taken over by mining and logging companies. They cut down large parts of the forest, forcing local people to move elsewhere.

▶ Embera women clean and prepare food in rivers and lakes, but many have become polluted.

Forests of Oceania

332 Hundreds of millions of years ago there was a giant continent called Gondwana. Around 140 million years ago, Gondwana began to split, and eventually Australia, New Zealand and New Guinea broke away from the rest of the landmass. Wildlife that evolved in these places is very different from that found elsewhere.

333 Walking through the cloud forests of New Guinea is an incredible experience. The air is damp, and every surface is covered with plants, especially mosses and ferns. When the clouds open, torrential rain drenches each living thing.

334 Dragons live in Australia's rainforest, waiting to pounce on passers-by. These are not real dragons, but lizards called Boyd's forest dragons – and they attack bugs, not people! They live on trees, where their patterned scales help them to stay hidden from view.

▶ Australian tree kangaroos scamper through branches. When they are scared, they can jump down from trees in one giant leap.

I DON'T BELIEVE IT!

In the last 200 years most of Australia's rainforests have been replaced by farms and towns. If the southern cassowary, an endangered bird of this region, becomes extinct, so will around 150 rainforest plants that rely on it to spread their seeds.

▼ Korowai families live in tall tree houses. They eat sago (from plants) beetle grubs, and hunt wild pigs.

◀ Boyd's dragon lizards sit motionless, waiting for prey to pass by, then pounce at speed.

335 **During the last Ice Age, rivers of ice (glaciers) covered parts of New Zealand.** Today the climate is warmer so wet and cool rainforests have replaced the glaciers. New Zealand's Fiordland forest is home to the Takahe parrot, which has lost the ability to fly because it had no natural predators in its forest home.

336 **Tribal people on the island of New Guinea live in homes up to 50 metres off the ground.** The tree houses built by tribes such as the Korowai and Kombai provide safety against warring tribes or dangerous creatures, especially disease-carrying mosquitoes.

Magical Madagascar

337 Madagascar is the world's fourth largest island. It lies to the east of Africa, in the warm waters of the Indian Ocean. The rainforests here cover 10,000 square kilometres, and are mostly found on the island's eastern coast.

338 When Madagascar split away from the rest of Africa about 165 million years ago, its animals and plants began moving on a unique path of change. Now this tropical place is a haven for some amazing animals such as lemurs and coloured lizards called chameleons. Between 80 and 90 percent of the 250,000 species found here live nowhere else, and new species are discovered all the time.

▼ Ring-tailed lemurs live together in groups that are ruled by females. They feed on plants and, unlike most lemurs, spend much of their time on the ground.

339 Lemurs are animals with long legs and bushy tails that leap through trees. They are related to monkeys and apes and, like their cousins, are intelligent and inquisitive creatures. The ring-tailed lemur lives in groups of up to 25 family members. They like to sit in the sun, but scatter if a member of the group sounds an alarm call to warn of danger nearby.

◀ The wings of the African sunset moth are ablaze with beautiful colours. Like most colourful moths, it is active during the day.

340 People have been living on Madagascar for around 2000 years. Travellers from Arabia, Asia, Africa and Indonesia have all settled here, along with Europeans. Four out of every five adults earns a living from agriculture. More than 90 percent of Madagascar's rainforests have been destroyed to provide farmland for the growing population.

◀ The rosy periwinkle is used to make drugs that fight deadly diseases.

341 The pretty rosy periwinkle plant is found in Madagascar's rainforests and is used to fight cancer. It contains chemicals that are used to make drugs that combat this deadly disease. The rosy periwinkle is endangered in the wild because its forest home has been largely destroyed.

I DON'T BELIEVE IT!

Lemurs in Madagascar have been seen rolling giant millipedes over their fur. No one knew why, until scientists discovered that the many-legged bugs release chemicals that keep flies and fleas off the lemurs – like a natural fly spray!

▶ A Madagascan aye-aye taps a tree with its long middle finger. It listens for sounds of moving grubs beneath, and hooks them out.

151

African adventures

342 The Congo rainforest (or Central African rainforest) lies in the centre of Africa, in the basin of the Congo River. It is the second largest rainforest, with an area around twice the size of France. More than 50 million people depend on it for survival.

▲ The Central African rainforest is home to more than 11,000 types of plant and 400 types of mammal, such as African forest elephants.

344 Walking through the African rainforest is a challenging, frightening, noisy activity! Plants block every step and strange noises come from all corners, including squeaks, trilling, singing, cheeps, growls and roars. Deadly snakes and spiders lurk in dark corners, and biting or stinging insects will sniff out human flesh in seconds.

343 Before European explorers ventured into Africa's jungles the native people lived in harmony with their environment. They survived as hunter-gatherers – they only killed what they needed to eat, and collected fruits by hand. Europeans wanted to use the rainforests to make money – a practice that continues today.

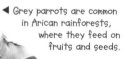

◄ Grey parrots are common in Arican rainforests, where they feed on fruits and seeds.

345

The Batwa people of Central Africa are pygmies, which means they are unusually short. They have lived in African rainforests for thousands of years, collecting honey and hunting. When farmers destroyed the Batwas' forests, they were left without homes and with no way to get food. Most now live in great poverty.

► Some Batwa men still climb trees to collect honey, but most members of the tribe have been forced to leave their forest homes.

346

African hardwoods are prized for their great beauty and durability. These woods come from tropical trees and have been used for centuries to make fine furniture and decorative objects. Mahogany, ebony and teak are all exotic woods from African rainforests.

▼ Around 90 percent of the rainforests in West Africa have been wiped out by farming.

QUIZ

Three of these countries are in Africa, and three are in South America. Can you put them in the right continents?

Colombia Gabon Congo
Guyana Brazil Ghana

Answers:
Africa: Congo Gabon Ghana
South America: Brazil Colombia
Guyana

Forests of the Far East

347 The word 'jungle' comes from a Hindi word meaning 'thick forest'. Most Asian rainforests lie on the mainland, from India to Bhutan and Malaysia, or on tropical islands such as Sumatra.

▼Orang-utans live in trees, but they do spend some time on land. They can walk through water, but do not swim.

348 Borneo cloud forests provide shelter and food for one of the world's most endangered apes. Orang-utans live in trees and feed on the fruit of more than 400 different types of tree, especially durians and figs. If they can't find fruit, they eat leaves and bark.

349 Palm trees provide an important source of food – sago.

Women make it from palm pith (the spongy substance inside a trunk or branch). They chop and soak it, before treading on it to turn it into a pulp. The pulp dries to a flour that can be cooked. Tribal people also enjoy delicious sago grubs – the large maggots that live inside rotting palm trees.

Powerful, curved beak

◀ The Philippine eagle has a wingspan of more than 2 metres and is a formidable predator, catching prey such as flying lemurs in mid-flight. It is in danger of extinction because more than 90 percent of its Philippine forest home has been cut down.

Sharp talons

RAIN RECORD

It rains almost every day in a rainforest. To measure your rainfall you need a clear plastic container, a ruler and a notebook.
1. Place the empty container outside, away from trees.
2. At the same time every day measure the water in the container.
3. Empty your container after each measurement.
4. Record your results in a notebook.

350 The people of the Indonesian rainforests are called Orang Asli and they have had a hard battle for survival in recent times.

In Malaysia, they were often captured and sold as slaves to local chiefs. Many Orang Asli still live in the rainforests, hunting monkeys with blowpipes made from bamboo.

Flying lemur

351 Known as the lord of the jungle, the Philippine eagle soars over Asian rainforests, hunting monkeys and squirrels.

It is one of the world's biggest raptors (birds of prey), but also one of the most endangered. There are now probably no more than 500 alive.

Cloud forests

352 Trekking through the Monteverde cloud forest of Costa Rica can be done on foot – or by air! Visitors can fly between the trees on zip wires, passing through low-lying clouds to get a bird's-eye view of the treetops. On the ground, every surface is wet, as it is either drizzling or pouring with rain for much of the day.

▲ Three-toed sloths are slow-moving mammals. Their camouflage is their only defence against jaguars – the big cats of South America that hunt them.

▼ Mountain gorillas live in the cloud forests of Africa's Virunga National Park. They are highly endangered animals, despite being our close cousins.

353 At night, cloud forests buzz with life, but the sleepy sloth rarely stirs. These animals from Central and South America are such slow movers that plants grow in their fur, giving perfect camouflage! Three-toed sloths hang from branches and sleep upside-down for up to 18 hours every day, only coming down to the ground once a week. It takes them one minute to travel just 3 metres.

354 Epiphytes are rainforest plants that grow very well in cloud forests. They emerge from the nooks and crannies of tree trunks and branches, to reach more sunlight than they would on the forest floor. Dirt collects in these places and turns to soil. The epiphytes' roots grow into this soil, where they collect nutrients and water.

▲ Trees in cloud forests are covered in epiphytes and they grow roots from their trunks and branches. These hanging roots can be tens of metres in length and absorb water from the damp atmosphere.

◄ In the mating season a male quetzal grows two tail feathers that may reach one metre in length.

GO SLOW

Measure out 3 metres on the floor. How quickly can you cover this distance when you run? Probably very quickly! Now try to cover the same distance as slowly as you can, so it takes a whole minute — just like a three-toed sloth. Now do it again, upside down (only joking!)

355 As a resplendent quetzal flies through Mexico's cloud forest its tail feathers shimmer in the sunlight. Male quetzals, known as birds of the gods, have the longest tail feathers of any bird in the region, and they are often regarded as one of the world's most beautiful birds. Quetzals eat wild avocados, swallowing the fruit whole. The seeds pass through their bodies, helping new avocado trees to grow.

Peculiar plants

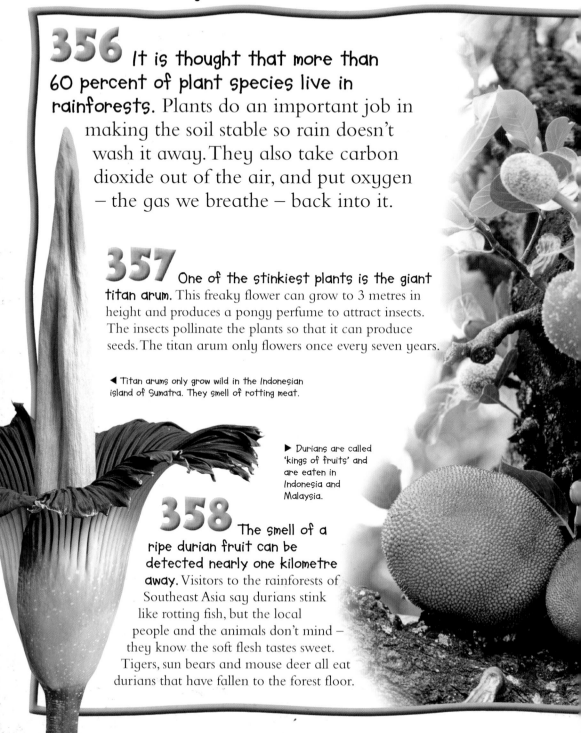

356 **It is thought that more than 60 percent of plant species live in rainforests.** Plants do an important job in making the soil stable so rain doesn't wash it away. They also take carbon dioxide out of the air, and put oxygen – the gas we breathe – back into it.

357 **One of the stinkiest plants is the giant titan arum.** This freaky flower can grow to 3 metres in height and produces a pongy perfume to attract insects. The insects pollinate the plants so that it can produce seeds. The titan arum only flowers once every seven years.

◀ Titan arums only grow wild in the Indonesian island of Sumatra. They smell of rotting meat.

▶ Durians are called 'kings of fruits' and are eaten in Indonesia and Malaysia.

358 **The smell of a ripe durian fruit can be detected nearly one kilometre away.** Visitors to the rainforests of Southeast Asia say durians stink like rotting fish, but the local people and the animals don't mind – they know the soft flesh tastes sweet. Tigers, sun bears and mouse deer all eat durians that have fallen to the forest floor.

▶ Look inside a pitcher plant and you can see how it traps bugs.

Slippery surface

Insects caught in thick liquid

359 **Pitcher plants are killers.** These pretty green plants lure bugs using a tempting scent. As insects land on the rim of the pitcher, their feet lose their grip on the waxy surface, sending them tumbling into the trap. The plant produces acid, which digests the insect's body, dissolving it within hours. The enormous rajah pitcher plant can even digest mice and birds!

360 **The biggest flower on Earth — the rafflesia — grows in the rainforests of Borneo.** This monster bloom can reach one metre across and smells of rotting flesh. The rafflesia lives on other plants and steals its food and water from its 'host'.

▶ Rafflesia plants are parasites so they do not need roots, stems or leaves. Their foul smell attracts flies that pollinate the flowers.

On the move

◄ Green vine snakes live in Southeast Asia and mostly prey upon frogs and lizards.

361 Moving through a rainforest is difficult. Trees, roots and shrubs fill every space, and there are few natural paths, so animals have to fly, swing, crawl or leap to find food, shelter and mates.

362 Walking in a jungle at night is especially challenging, as an inky darkness descends when the sun sets. Animals that hunt at night are called nocturnal. Some bats use echolocation – a type of sixth sense – to hunt and find their way through the web of branches, while others, such as flying foxes, use their exceptional eyesight.

363 Green vine snakes have pencil-thin bodies and can move between branches soundlessly, reaching up to one metre between trees. With their tails firmly wrapped around a branch these snakes dangle down, looking for prey they can catch with a single venomous bite.

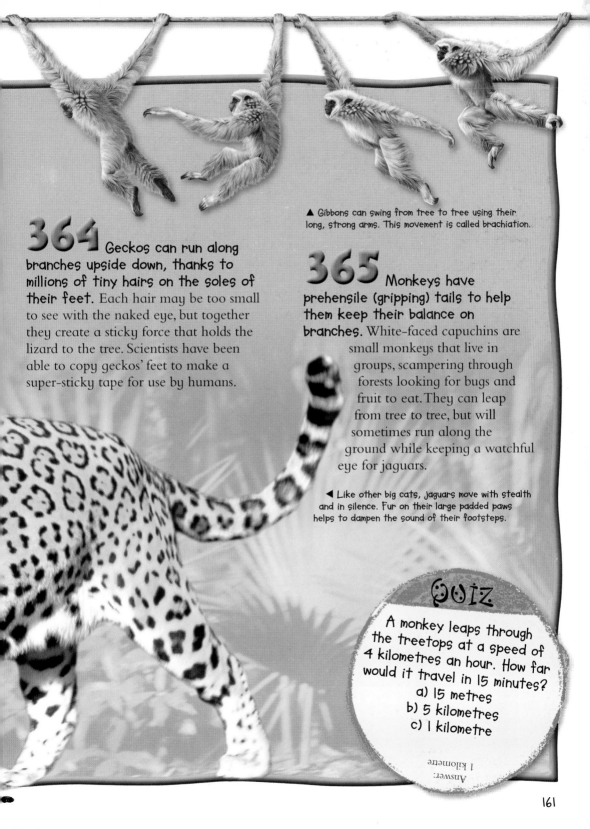

▲ Gibbons can swing from tree to tree using their long, strong arms. This movement is called brachiation.

364 Geckos can run along branches upside down, thanks to millions of tiny hairs on the soles of their feet. Each hair may be too small to see with the naked eye, but together they create a sticky force that holds the lizard to the tree. Scientists have been able to copy geckos' feet to make a super-sticky tape for use by humans.

365 Monkeys have prehensile (gripping) tails to help them keep their balance on branches. White-faced capuchins are small monkeys that live in groups, scampering through forests looking for bugs and fruit to eat. They can leap from tree to tree, but will sometimes run along the ground while keeping a watchful eye for jaguars.

◄ Like other big cats, jaguars move with stealth and in silence. Fur on their large padded paws helps to dampen the sound of their footsteps.

QUIZ

A monkey leaps through the treetops at a speed of 4 kilometres an hour. How far would it travel in 15 minutes?
a) 15 metres
b) 5 kilometres
c) 1 kilometre

Answer:
1 kilometre

Fantastic feathers

366 **Birds of paradise are the jewels in a rainforest crown.** These animals are dressed in feathers of fine colours and are adorned with crests, ruffs and streamers. Males use their bright, bold plumage to catch the attention of females, but they also do splendid dances and displays to make sure they can't be ignored!

367 **The mating dance of the male cock-of-the-rock is one of nature's most extraordinary sights.** Groups of males, with their bright-orange heads, collect on a branch near the forest floor, and put on a performance for a watching female. They flutter their wings, bob their heads and scuttle along the branch. The female mates with the male whose show has most impressed her.

▼ Male cocks-of-the-rock never hide themselves behind dull colours. Their startling plumage catches the attention of females — and predators.

368 **Wilson's bird of paradise has bare blue skin on its head, which is so bright it can be seen at night.** Males prepare a patch of ground to use as a stage, clearing it of all leaves and twigs. Their tails contain two skinny, curly silver feathers and their backs are metallic green. Like all birds of paradise, the females are not as brightly coloured as their mates.

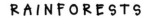

▼ When a male Raggiana bird of paradise is resting, its fan of orange-red feathers is hidden from view, but if a female nears, it will show itself in all its glory.

369 Birds of paradise live in Australia, New Guinea and some Asian islands. When dead samples of these birds were sent to Europe hundreds of years ago, their legs had been removed. This led scientists to believe that these creatures had come straight from paradise, and could not touch the ground until death, which is how they got their name.

Kaleidoscope of colour

370 Rainforests are full of shades of green, but the animals that live in them are often bold and bright in colour. Strong colours help animals send signals to one another in a habitat where it is easy to be hidden from view.

Postman butterfly

Birdwing butterfly

Blue morpho butterfly

▲ The wings of many butterflies are covered in tiny scales that reflect light rays to create a range of shimmering colours.

▶ A strawberry poison-dart frog from Costa Rica has bright colours to warn of the poison it has on its skin.

371 While some animals use colour to draw attention to themselves, others use it to hide. Giant stick insects, like many other bugs in the forest, are patterned in mottled shades of green, grey or brown so they blend in with their surroundings. Camouflage is one way to avoid being eaten in the jungle, but there are many other ways to stay alive.

◀ The giant stick insect can reach 45 centimetres in length.

Parasol fungi

372 The forest floor is littered with brightly coloured 'umbrellas'. These little growths, called toadstools or mushrooms, are fungi – living things that are similar to plants but do not need sunlight. Orange, gold, red, blue and yellow are common fungi colours, which may alert grazing animals to the poisons they contain.

Cup fungi

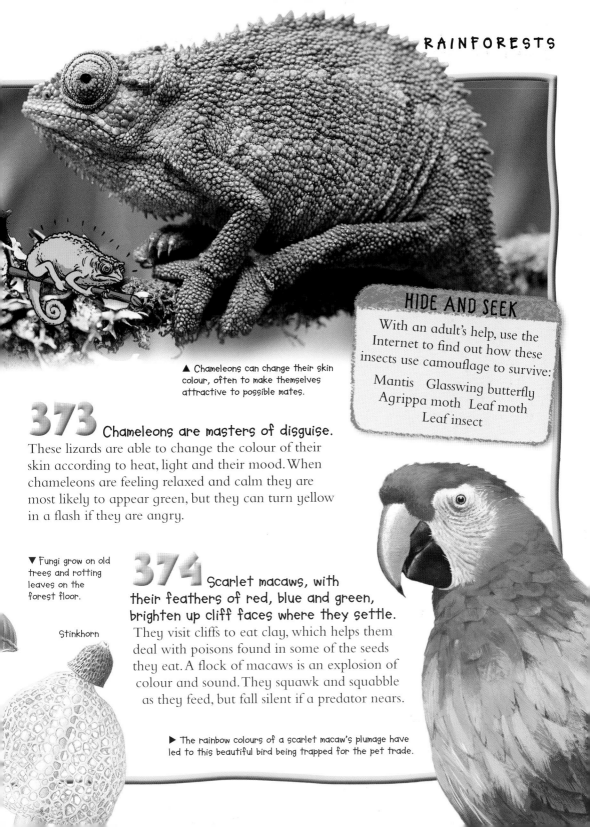

▲ Chameleons can change their skin colour, often to make themselves attractive to possible mates.

HIDE AND SEEK

With an adult's help, use the Internet to find out how these insects use camouflage to survive:

Mantis   Glasswing butterfly
Agrippa moth   Leaf moth
Leaf insect

373 **Chameleons are masters of disguise.**
These lizards are able to change the colour of their skin according to heat, light and their mood. When chameleons are feeling relaxed and calm they are most likely to appear green, but they can turn yellow in a flash if they are angry.

▼ Fungi grow on old trees and rotting leaves on the forest floor.

Stinkhorn

374 **Scarlet macaws, with their feathers of red, blue and green, brighten up cliff faces where they settle.**
They visit cliffs to eat clay, which helps them deal with poisons found in some of the seeds they eat. A flock of macaws is an explosion of colour and sound. They squawk and squabble as they feed, but fall silent if a predator nears.

▶ The rainbow colours of a scarlet macaw's plumage have led to this beautiful bird being trapped for the pet trade.

The key to survival

375 Surviving in a rainforest is a battle for most animals. Food and shelter are plentiful, but habitats are so crowded it is easy for predators to hide. As a result, many creatures have developed amazing ways to stay alive.

376 Some rainforest animals pretend to be poisonous. When explorer Henry Bates (1825–1892) examined butterflies in the Amazon he found one type of patterned butterfly that tasted foul to birds, and another type that looked very similar, which didn't. He concluded that some animals copy (mimic), the appearance of others that are poisonous to avoid being eaten.

▲ Leaflitter toads are named for their clever camouflage. They resemble the decaying leaves of their forest floor habitat.

▼ Goliath tarantulas don't build webs to catch their prey – they hunt just like bigger predators, stalking animals such as frogs.

377 Poisons are common in many rainforest creatures. However, the Goliath tarantula spider uses flying hairs, as well as poisons, to keep safe! Probably the world's largest spider, it reaches 30 centimetres across, with 2.5-centimetre-long fangs. If threatened, Goliath tarantula spiders shoot hairs at attackers, which cause irritation and pain.

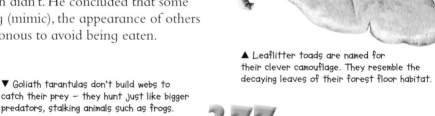

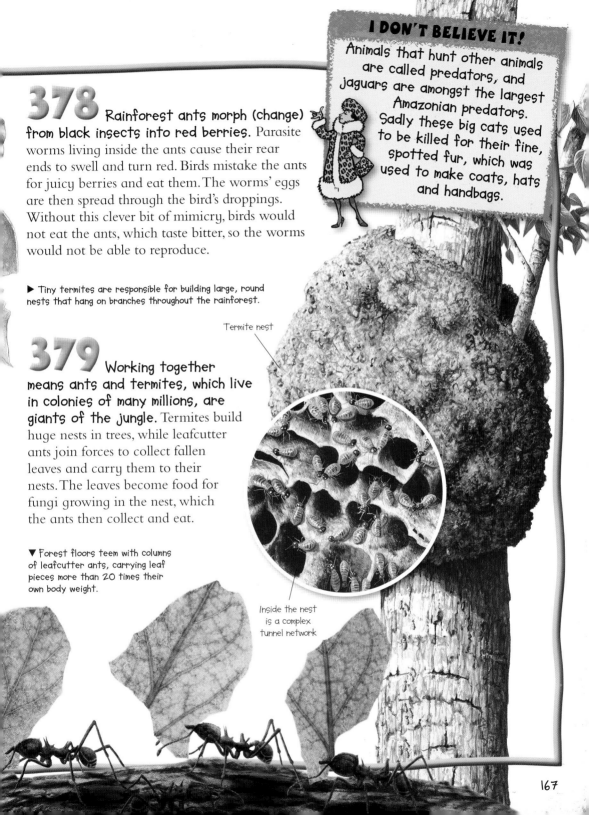

I DON'T BELIEVE IT!

Animals that hunt other animals are called predators, and jaguars are amongst the largest Amazonian predators. Sadly these big cats used to be killed for their fine, spotted fur, which was used to make coats, hats and handbags.

378 Rainforest ants morph (change) from black insects into red berries. Parasite worms living inside the ants cause their rear ends to swell and turn red. Birds mistake the ants for juicy berries and eat them. The worms' eggs are then spread through the bird's droppings. Without this clever bit of mimicry, birds would not eat the ants, which taste bitter, so the worms would not be able to reproduce.

▶ Tiny termites are responsible for building large, round nests that hang on branches throughout the rainforest.

Termite nest

379 Working together means ants and termites, which live in colonies of many millions, are giants of the jungle. Termites build huge nests in trees, while leafcutter ants join forces to collect fallen leaves and carry them to their nests. The leaves become food for fungi growing in the nest, which the ants then collect and eat.

▼ Forest floors teem with columns of leafcutter ants, carrying leaf pieces more than 20 times their own body weight.

Inside the nest is a complex tunnel network

167

The jungle's bounty

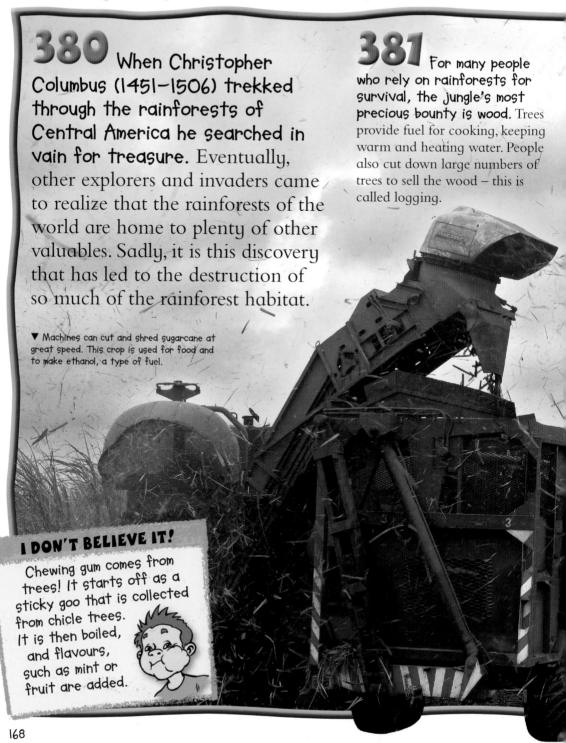

380 When Christopher Columbus (1451–1506) trekked through the rainforests of Central America he searched in vain for treasure. Eventually, other explorers and invaders came to realize that the rainforests of the world are home to plenty of other valuables. Sadly, it is this discovery that has led to the destruction of so much of the rainforest habitat.

▼ Machines can cut and shred sugarcane at great speed. This crop is used for food and to make ethanol, a type of fuel.

381 For many people who rely on rainforests for survival, the jungle's most precious bounty is wood. Trees provide fuel for cooking, keeping warm and heating water. People also cut down large numbers of trees to sell the wood – this is called logging.

I DON'T BELIEVE IT!

Chewing gum comes from trees! It starts off as a sticky goo that is collected from chicle trees. It is then boiled, and flavours, such as mint or fruit are added.

▲ Cocoa beans grow inside pods.

▲ Latex drips into a collecting cup.

▲ Star fruits, or carambolas, can be sweet or sour.

382
Chocolate, sugar and rubber come from rainforest plants. Cocoa pods are cut open to reveal seeds (cocoa beans) which are dried, cleaned and made into chocolate. Sugar comes from a grass called sugarcane that grows in tropical areas. Rubber is harvested from trees as a white sticky gum called latex, which is made into many useful products such as tyres and hoses.

384
Many delicious fruits, vegetables, nuts, spices and herbs come from rainforests, although they may be cultivated (grown) in other places. Shops around the world sell ginger, cloves, pepper, nutmeg, pineapples, bananas, starfruits and sweet potatoes, all of which originally came from rainforests.

383
Scientists are discovering that rainforest plants can be used to treat diseases. The people of the rainforests have known this for thousands of years. Quinine is a chemical that comes from the bark of the cinchona tree. It has been used by Amazonian Indians to prevent malaria – a deadly disease spread by mosquitoes. It is thought many rainforest plants could be used to treat cancer in the future.

▶ The outer bark of a cinchona tree is peeled back to reveal yellow inner bark, which contains quinine.

Paradise lost

385 Mangrove forests are one of the world's fastest disappearing habitats. Half of them have been destroyed in just 50 years. The trees are cut down so the swampy ground can be used to cultivate shrimps to be sold as food. Coastal areas that have lost their mangrove forests are more likely to suffer from tsunamis, storms and flooding.

386 The red-vented cockatoo is one of the world's rarest birds. Chicks are taken from nests and sold as pets – there may now be as few as 1000 left. The giant elephant birds of Madagascar died out centuries ago when their eggs were taken for food.

387 Gold mines, which use the poisonous metal mercury, have been established in some rainforests. Water that contains mercury can kill anything that comes into contact with it, and may have caused the disappearance of many types of frog and toad.

▲ This mangrove swamp in Indonesia has been devastated by shrimp farming. Mangroves protect land from water damage and are home to many animals, which, once destroyed, may take centuries to recover.

388
Humans' closest relatives are being eaten to extinction. Primates such as gorillas, chimps and bonobos are sold as meat in Africa, while monkeys and langurs are served as luxury dishes in Asia. Primates also suffer when their habitats are affected by human conflicts.

▲ WWF international staff patrols search for evidence of poaching activities in central Africa.

389
When the forest dies, so does a way of life. Now the future looks uncertain for millions of tribal people whose families have depended on rainforests for centuries. When they lose their forest homes, it is hard for people to retain the knowledge and skills that help them to survive.

▶ Wild populations of great apes such as chimpanzees are disappearing fast.

Burning issues

390
Cutting down forests is called deforestation. Many forests are lost when they are turned into plantations – large fields that are used to grow single crops, such as bananas or rubber. Scientists believe that at least 19 million precious rainforest trees are cut down every day for wood or to make way for crops.

391
Around one-sixth of the Amazon rainforest has been destroyed, yet deforestation continues around the world. New roads are being built in the South American and African rainforests, which make it easier to fell trees. As many countries with rainforests are poor, selling wood can seem a good way for people to pay for food.

▼ It only takes a few hours for modern machines to fell trees and remove vegetation so the land can be used for farming.

I DON'T BELIEVE IT!
Orang-utans are close to extinction because their forests are becoming palm plantations. Palm oil is used in food and as a fuel. It is expected that orang-utans will be gone from the wild in less than ten years.

▲ Aerial photos show how huge areas of rainforest are being destroyed so the land can be used for cattle and crops.

▼ Slash and burn is used to clear the ground. When it is done too often, or over a large area, entire habitats may be changed or destroyed forever.

392 The Amazon rainforest is being cut down to provide land for cattle. These animals are used for beef, which is sent to developed nations for use in hamburgers and similar foods. There are more than 200 million herds of cattle in the region, and that number is likely to grow.

393 Large areas of rainforest are destroyed using 'slash and burn'. Trees and plants are cut down, and the remains are burned. The cleared ground is used for growing crops, or as land for cattle. This method of deforestation ruins the soil, so the farmers then have to move on to a new patch of forest.

394 Deforestation has been found to affect our atmosphere and climate. Removing these massive ecosystems could cause droughts and flooding. Once forests are gone, the soil is not held together so well, causing soil erosion, so landslides become more common and plants can no longer grow.

Forests for the future

395 We must preserve the world's rainforests if we value the people and wildlife that live in them. Less than eight percent of these ecosystems are currently strictly protected from deforestation, but governments could turn rainforests into national parks so they cannot be used for farming or logging.

▲ Tourists pay to go on canopy walks and admire the rainforests from above. Money from tourism can be used to protect these habitats and give local people jobs.

▼ Solar panels collect the Sun's energy, which can be turned into electrical energy to provide light and heat.

396 Rainforest people can be shown how to use solar power to produce energy for light and cooking. Solar power is sustainable, which means it will never run out – unlike rainforest trees. Wood fires produce dirty smoke, but solar energy, which comes from the sun, is pollution-free.

397 Technology may help save the Congo rainforest in Africa. Local people who find better ways to earn money than cutting down trees will be helped with money from a special fund. Their progress will be checked using satellite images of the forest.

398 It was once thought that when a rainforest had gone, it would be gone forever. However, scientists have grown a fresh forest in Borneo to replace one that has been destroyed. Seeds from more than 1300 trees were planted, and the soil was treated with a special fertilizer. Now 30 types of mammal and 116 types of bird have moved in. Local people have been involved with the project, and helped it to succeed.

▶ Workers at an orang-utan orphanage in Borneo care for baby orangs that have lost their parents to hunting or the illegal pet trade.

399 Everyone can make a difference to the future of the rainforests. Shoppers can check they are not buying products that come from rainforest regions, and governments can develop tourism so that local people can earn a living protecting forests, rather than destroying them.

Products that may come from rainforest regions:

* Wood   * Beef
* Soya   * Palm oil

Check labels before buying

400 Rainforests will only be preserved if people respect all of Earth's delicate ecosystems. Everyone who cares about nature hopes that there is still time to halt the damage, and that rainforests will still be around in the centuries to come.

The Earth in danger

401 **Our planet is in a mess!** Humans have done more damage to the Earth than any other species. We take over land for farms, cities and roads, we hunt animals until they die out and we produce waste and pollution. Gases from cars, power stations and factories are changing the atmosphere and making the planet heat up. By making a few changes to live in a 'greener' way, we can try to save our planet.

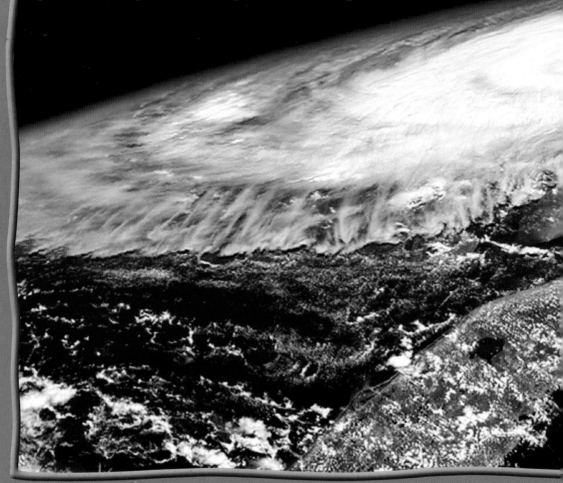

▼ As pollution makes the Earth warm up, more powerful storms form over the sea. This satellite photo shows Hurricane Frances moving over the Caribbean in 2004.

Global warming

Some heat gets trapped by the layer of gases

Sun

Some heat escapes back into space

Layer of gases

▲ Global warming happens when greenhouse gases collect in the Earth's atmosphere. They let heat from the Sun through, but as it bounces back, it gets trapped close to the Earth, making the planet heat up.

402 **Throughout its history, the Earth has warmed up and cooled down.** Experts think that today's warming is down to humans – and it's happening faster than normal. Carbon dioxide and methane gases are released into the air as pollution. They are known as greenhouse gases and can stop the Sun's heat escaping from the atmosphere.

403 **Global warming tells us that the climate is changing.** Weather changes every day – we have hot days and cold days – but on average the climate is warming up. Scientists think that average temperatures have risen by one degree Celsius in the last 100 years, and that they will keep rising.

I DON'T BELIEVE IT!

Scientists think that sea levels could rise by one metre by 2100 – maybe even more. Three million years ago when the Earth was hotter, the sea was 200 metres higher than today. We could be heading that way again.

404 **Warmer temperatures mean wilder weather.** Wind happens when air is heated and gets lighter. It rises up and cold air is sucked in to replace it. Rain occurs when heat makes water in rivers and seas turn into vapour in the air. It rises up and forms rain clouds. Warmer temperatures mean more wind, rain and storms.

KEY

☐ Average area of sea covered by ice from 1980–2000

☐ Predicted area of sea covered by ice for 2080–2100

ARCTIC OCEAN

◄ The ice in the Arctic Ocean is melting so fast that scientists think over half of it could be gone by 2100.

▼ Huge chunks of ice often break off into the sea at Paradise Bay, at the Antarctic.

405 As the Earth heats up, its ice melts. Vast areas of the Earth are covered in ice. It is found around the North and South Poles, and on high mountains. Now, because of global warming, more and more of this ice is melting. It turns into water and flows into the sea. Also, as the water gets warmer, it expands (gets bigger) and the sea takes up more space, making sea levels rise.

▶ Polar bears depend on large chunks of ice to hunt and rest on. Melting ice in the Arctic is making life much harder for them.

Energy crisis

406
We pump greenhouse gases into the atmosphere because we burn fuels to make energy. Cars, planes and trains run on fuel, and we also burn it in power stations to produce electricity. The main fuels – coal, oil and gas – are called fossil fuels because they formed underground over millions of years.

▶ Oil and natural gas formed from the remains of tiny prehistoric sea creatures that collected on the seabed. Layers of rock built up on top and squashed them. Over time, they became underground stores of oil, with pockets of gas above.

407
Fossil fuels are running out. Because they take so long to form, we are using up fossil fuels much faster than they can be replaced. Eventually, they will become so rare that it will be too expensive to find them. Experts think this will happen before the end of the 21st century.

Oil platform drilling for oil and gas

Hard rock layer

Gas

Oil

Oil and gas move upwards through soft rock layers until reaching a hard rock layer

The layer of dead sea creatures is crushed by rock that forms above, and turns into oil and gas

Tiny sea creatures die and sink to the seabed

408
One thing we can do is find other fuels. Besides fossil fuels, we can burn fuels that come from plants. For example, the rape plant contains oil that can be burned in vehicle engines. However, burning these fuels still releases greenhouse gases.

409 Nuclear power is another kind of energy. By splitting apart atoms – the tiny units that all materials are made of – energy is released, which can be turned into electricity. However, producing this energy creates toxic waste that can make people ill, and may be accidentally released into the air. Safer ways to use nuclear power are being researched.

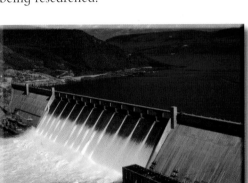

▲ The Grand Coulee Dam in Washington, USA, holds back a river, creating a lake, or reservoir. Water is let through the dam to turn turbines, which create electricity.

410 Lots of energy is produced without burning anything. Hydroelectric power stations use the pushing power of flowing rivers to turn turbines. Hydroelectricity is a renewable, or green, energy source – it doesn't use anything up or cause pollution. Scientists are also working on ways to turn the movement of waves and tides into usable energy.

411 The wind and the Sun are great renewable sources of energy, too. Wind turbines turn generators, which convert the 'turning movement' into electricity. Solar panels work by collecting sunlight and turning it into an electrical current.

Rotor blade

◄ Solar panels are made of materials that soak up sunlight and turn its energy into a flow of electricity.

▲ Modern wind turbines usually have three blades, which spin around at speed in high winds.

On the move

412 **Cars release a lot of greenhouse gases.** No one had a car 200 years ago. Now, there are around 500 million cars in the world and most are used daily. Cars burn petrol or diesel, which are made from oil – a fossil fuel. We can reduce greenhouse gases and slow down global warming by using cars less.

Carbon dioxide (CO_2)

Nitrogen dioxide (NO_2)

Sulphur dioxide (SO_2)

▲ Car exhaust fumes contain harmful, polluting gases, including sulphur dioxide, nitrogen dioxide and carbon dioxide, which are poisonous to humans.

▼ In many cities, there are so many cars that they cause big traffic jams. They move slowly with their engines running, churning out even more pollution.

413 **Public transport is made up of buses, trams and trains that everyone can use.** It's a greener way to travel than by car. Buses can carry 60 or 70 people at once and trains can carry several hundred. They still burn fuel, but release much less greenhouse gases per person.

COUNT YOUR STEPS

Besides saving on greenhouse gases, walking is great exercise and helps you stay healthy. Try counting your steps for one whole day. How many can you do – 3000, 5000 or even 10,000?

414 **Planes fly long distances at high speeds, giving out tonnes of greenhouse gases on each journey.** A return flight from the UK to the USA releases more carbon dioxide than a car does in one year. Where you can, travel by boat or train for shorter journeys.

▶ Maglev trains use magnets to hover above the rails. The magnetic force propels the train forward, rather than a petrol- or diesel-burning engine.

▲ Cyclists in Beijing, China, enjoy World Car-Free Day. This was organized to help reduce pollution.

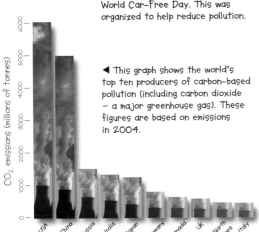

◀ This graph shows the world's top ten producers of carbon-based pollution (including carbon dioxide – a major greenhouse gas). These figures are based on emissions in 2004.

415 **The greenest way to get around is to walk.** For short journeys, walk instead of going by car. Inside buildings, use the stairs instead of taking lifts and escalators. Cycling is good, too. A bicycle doesn't burn any fuels, it just uses the power of your legs.

416 **Long ago, before engines and turbines were invented, transport worked differently.** Boats had sails or oars and were driven by wind or human power, and carts and carriages were pulled by animals. As fossil fuels run out, we may see some old means of transport coming back.

Save energy at home

417 Saving electricity at home reduces pollution. Most electricity we use is produced from burning fossil fuels. By using less of it, we can cut greenhouse gas emissions. Always turn off lights, TVs, computers and other electrical devices when not in use. Low-energy light bulbs are a good idea, too. They use less power and last longer.

▼ Washing hung outside dries in the heat of the Sun. This saves on electricity and fossil fuels.

419 We invent all kinds of electrical gadgets to do things for us, but do we really need them? You can save energy by sweeping the floor instead of using a vacuum cleaner every time. Use your hands to make bread, instead of a food processor. Avoid electrical can openers, knives and other power-hungry gadgets.

418 Your washing can be green as well as clean! Tumble dryers dry quickly, but they use lots of electricity. In summer, peg your clothes out on a washing line in the garden. In winter, hang them on a drier close to a radiator. You can save even more energy by washing clothes at a lower temperature, such as 30°C.

I DON'T BELIEVE IT!

Only 10 percent of the electricity used by an old-style light bulb is turned into light. The rest turns into wasted heat, which also makes it burn out quicker.

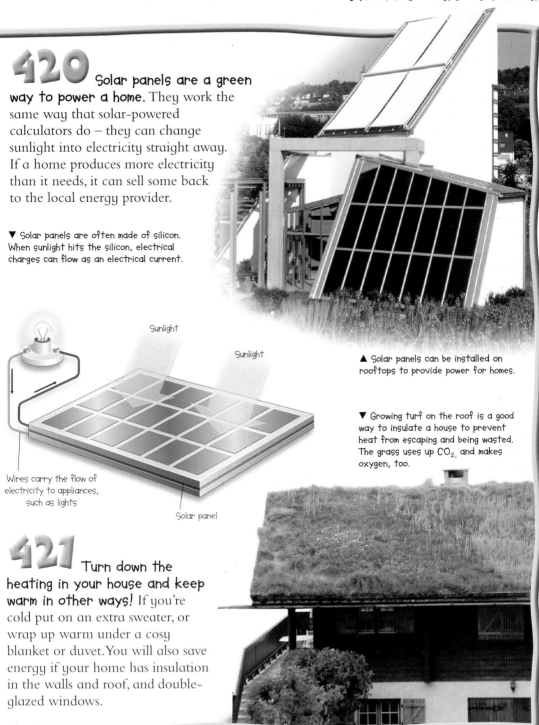

420

Solar panels are a green way to power a home. They work the same way that solar-powered calculators do – they can change sunlight into electricity straight away. If a home produces more electricity than it needs, it can sell some back to the local energy provider.

▼ Solar panels are often made of silicon. When sunlight hits the silicon, electrical charges can flow as an electrical current.

Sunlight

Sunlight

▲ Solar panels can be installed on rooftops to provide power for homes.

▼ Growing turf on the roof is a good way to insulate a house to prevent heat from escaping and being wasted. The grass uses up CO_2, and makes oxygen, too.

Wires carry the flow of electricity to appliances, such as lights

Solar panel

421

Turn down the heating in your house and keep warm in other ways! If you're cold put on an extra sweater, or wrap up warm under a cosy blanket or duvet. You will also save energy if your home has insulation in the walls and roof, and double-glazed windows.

Green shopping

422 **Most people buy something from a shop every day.** Items such as food, clothes and furniture take a lot of energy to grow, manufacture and then transport to the shops. By doing some smart shopping, you can save some of that energy.

▲ Old plastic bags fill up landfill sites and take hundreds of years to rot away. They can also harm wildlife.

▶ Bags made from cloth can be used over and over again.

423 **Say no to plastic bags!** Plastic bags are made from oil – a fossil fuel – and it takes energy to make them. However, we often use them once then throw them away, which creates litter and pollution. When you go shopping take a re-usable bag made from cloth, or re-use old plastic bags so that you don't have to use new ones.

424 **How far has your food travelled?** The distance food has been transported is called 'food miles'. You can reduce food miles by shopping at farm shops and local markets. In supermarkets, look at packages to find food that was produced nearby. Food that has travelled far is greener if it came by boat, and not by plane.

▲ On the island of Saint Vincent in the Caribbean, people buy bananas that have been grown locally. Bananas grown here are also shipped to other countries — a much greener way to transport than by plane.

425 **More and more people are buying bottled water.** Water is heavy and a lot of fuel is needed to transport it long distances. The plastic bottles create waste and cause pollution, too. It's greener to use clean, pure water from the tap at home.

▼ This paper shows that anything can be recycled! Roo Poo paper is made from 80 percent recycled paper and 20 percent kangaroo droppings.

GENUINE ROO POO PAPER

426 **Buying second-hand goods is a great way to save energy.** When you buy second-hand clothes, furniture or books nothing new has to be made in a factory. Antique furniture and vintage clothes are often better quality than new things and more individual, too.

Reduce, re-use, recycle

427 **Most of us buy more than we need.** We want the latest clothes, toys and cars even though we may not need them – this is called consumerism. Reduce, re-use and recycle is a good way to remember what we can do to reduce the amount of things we buy.

428 **To start with, reduce your shopping.** Do you or your family ever buy things that don't end up getting used? Next time, think before you buy – be sure that you are going to use it. Buying less means less things have to be made, transported and thrown away. It saves money, too!

▶ Recycling materials greatly reduces the amount of energy needed to make new products. This graph shows how much energy is saved in making new products using recycled materials, rather than raw materials.

Empty glass bottles go into a recycling bin

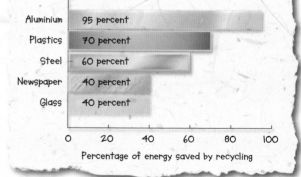

Aluminium	95 percent
Plastics	70 percent
Steel	60 percent
Newspaper	40 percent
Glass	40 percent

0 20 40 60 80 100

Percentage of energy saved by recycling

429 **Recycling means that materials can be made into new things instead of thrown away.** This saves energy and makes less waste. Paper, cardboard, food cans, glass and some plastics can all be recycled. Some local councils collect them, or you can take them to a recycling collection point at a school, supermarket or rubbish dump.

The bottles are collected from the bin and transported to a glass recycling plant

The old, broken glass is cleaned and melted down with other substances

430
We live in a 'throwaway society'. We are used to disposable things that get used once, then go in the bin. When something breaks, it's easy to get another, but making and transporting these new things uses up raw materials, and creates pollution. Re-use some of the things you throw away – mend clothes by sewing on a new button, pocket or patch and use empty food containers to store things in.

▼ These shopping bags have been made from old, recycled food sacks. They save on raw materials and cut down on plastic bags.

431
If you can't re-use something yourself, maybe someone else can. Give old clothes, furniture, books and toys to a charity shop, or sell them at a car boot sale or a fundraising jumble sale at school.

The bottles are sold and used, and can then be recycled again

▼ Recycled glass is used in road surfaces, concrete production, and a finely ground glass is used to fill golf bunkers. New bottles and jars are also made from recycled glass.

The bottles are filled with drinks and labelled

The liquid glass is blow moulded (blown with air) into new bottles

Green machines

432 As well as using machines less, we can use greener ones. Cars, computers and electrical appliances don't have to use lots of energy. Scientists are working on greener versions that use less electricity or fuel – or even none at all.

433 When hydrogen gas burns, it doesn't release any greenhouse gases – just water. Today, some cars run on hydrogen and create no pollution. However, making the hydrogen for them to run on uses up electricity, and in turn fossil fuels. As fossil fuels run out and renewable energy sources take over, hydrogen cars may become common.

I DON'T BELIEVE IT!

The fastest human-powered vehicles are recumbent cycles, which the rider drives in a lying-down position. They can travel at over 130 kilometres per hour.

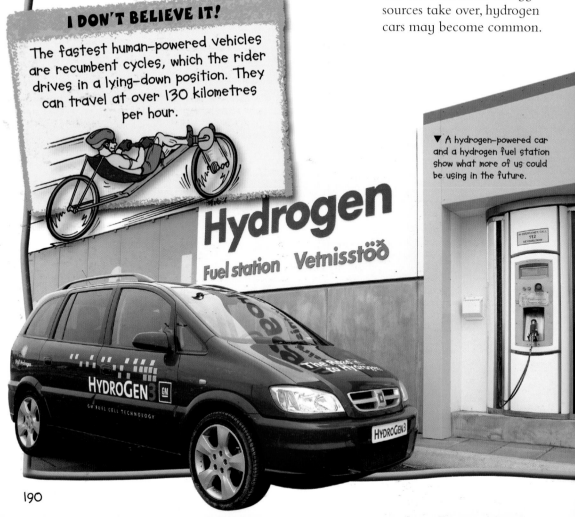

▼ A hydrogen-powered car and a hydrogen fuel station show what more of us could be using in the future.

Hydrogen
Fuel station Vetnisstöð

HYDROGEN3 GM
GM FUEL CELL TECHNOLOGY

HYDROGEN3

434 You might have travelled on an electric train or bus before. Instead of burning fuel, they run on electricity supplied from a large, on-board battery or overhead cables. This means less air pollution in city centres.

▲ Trams like this can be found in many cities around the world. They work by collecting electricity from overhead wires or cables.

435 Did you know that 'white goods' can be green? White goods are refrigerators, washing machines, dishwashers and other kitchen appliances. New ones have a rating showing how green they are. The greenest ones use the least energy and supplies such as water. Now you can choose the best ones for the planet.

▶ This solar-powered phone charger uses solar panels to turn sunlight into an electricity supply.

◀ As well as saving on electricity, wind-up radios are very useful in parts of the world where there is no electricity supply, such as parts of Africa.

436 Wind-up power was once used for toys, but now there are wind-up radios, torches and mobile phone chargers. The handle is wound and the energy from this movement is turned into an electricity supply inside the machine. Wind-up machines save on fossil fuels and reduce greenhouse gases.

Science solutions

▼ An artist's impression of a space shield that could be used to shade the Earth from the Sun.

437 Using less energy is one way to slow down global warming, but there might be others, too. Scientists are coming up with all kinds of space-age and hi-tech solutions that could help the Earth to cool down again.

438 Maybe we could shade the Earth to cool it down. Scientists have lots of ideas about how to do this. Some of these include launching huge mirrors into space to reflect the Sun's light and heat away, or filling the atmosphere with tiny particles to blot out the Sun. Another is to spread out a fine mesh, like a giant sheet, into space to make a sunshade. So far, all of these ideas are far too expensive to try.

I DON'T BELIEVE IT!

In a single day a cow can give out 500 litres of methane gas. That's enough to fill more than 100 party balloons!

192

▶ A huge cloud of green algae can be seen near the shore of Lake Tahoe, USA. Algae is made up of millions of tiny plants. There is so much algae in the world that it soaks up a lot of the world's carbon dioxide.

439 Instead of greenhouse gases filling the air, we could soak them up. Plants naturally take in carbon dioxide (CO_2) – a greenhouse gas – so planting lots of trees helps to slow global warming. Scientists are also trying to develop special types of algae (tiny plants) that can soak up even more greenhouse gases.

Sunlight

Sugars (food for the plant)

CO_2

Oxygen

Water

▲ Plants make food using sunlight, by a process called photosynthesis. They use up carbon dioxide and give out oxygen.

440 We could catch greenhouse gases before they escape into the air. There are already devices that can do this, which capture carbon dioxide from power stations and factory chimneys. Once it is caught, the gas needs to be stored safely. Scientists are looking at ways of storing carbon dioxide, or changing it into something harmless.

▼ A special foam wrapping is unrolled over the Tortin glacier in Switzerland to stop it melting.

441 As they digest grass, cows and other grazing animals pass a lot of wind! This gas contains methane – a greenhouse gas. Besides burning fuels, this is one of the biggest causes of global warming. Scientists are experimenting with feeding cows different foods to reduce the amount of methane.

Pollution problems

442 **Pollution means dirt, waste and other substances that damage our surroundings.** Our farms and factories often release harmful chemicals into rivers and lakes, and cars, lorries and other road vehicles give out poisonous, polluting gases. Litter and rubbish are pollution, too.

▼ A thick layer of smog hangs over the city of Bangkok, the capital of Thailand.

443 **Humans make waste — when we go to the toilet.** The waste and water from our toilets is called sewage. This usually ends up at sewage works where we process it to make it safe, but in some places sewage flows straight into rivers or the sea. It is smelly and dirty and can contain deadly germs.

444 **Pollution can harm our health.** Smog is a mixture of smoke from factories and motor vehicles, and fog, and it collects over some cities. It makes it harder to breathe, worsening illnesses such as asthma.

◄ People in Kuala Lumpur, the capital of Malaysia, wear masks to avoid breathing in smog.

◀ People who live near airports have to put up with the sound of low-flying planes flying over their houses.

445 Even noise is a kind of pollution.
Noise from airports disturbs the people who live nearby, and loud noises from ships and submarines can disturb whales. They rely on their own sounds to find their way and send messages, so other noises can confuse them.

446 The more we throw away, the more rubbish piles up.
When we drop rubbish just anywhere, it becomes litter. If we put rubbish in the bin, some of it may get recycled, and the rest gets taken away and dumped in a big hole in the ground, called a landfill site. Either way, there's too much of it!

▶ At landfill sites, rubbish piles up making huge mountains of waste that have to be flattened down by rollers.

447 Air pollution can cause acid rain.
The waste gases from power stations and factories mix with water droplets in clouds and form weak acid. This makes soil, rivers and lakes more acidic, which can kill fish and plants. Acid rain can even make rock crumble and dissolve.

TRUE OR FALSE?

1. Rubbish isn't a problem if you put it in a bin.
2. Acid rain can make your nose fall off.
3. Loud noises in the ocean can make whales get lost.

Answers:
1. FALSE – it still piles up in landfill sites. 2. FALSE – the acid is not very strong, but it can dissolve away the stone nose of a statue. 3. TRUE – according to some scientists.

195

Litter and rubbish

► Forest fires caused by dropped litter, such as glass bottles and cigarette ends, can be deadly and cost a lot of money to put out. Here, a helicopter drops water onto a forest fire.

448 **After leaving your house, rubbish has a long life ahead of it.** Things such as banana skins will rot away quickly, but man-made products such as plastics take a long time to decay and break down. That's why landfill sites fill up fast, and we have to find more and more space for our rubbish.

449 **A drinks bottle left in a dry field or forest could start a fire.** The curved glass in a bottle – especially a piece of a broken bottle – can act like a magnifying glass. If it focuses the Sun's heat on a dry patch of grass, a fire can start.

I DON'T BELIEVE IT!

People drop the most litter from cars because they think they can make a quick getaway! However, governments are making new laws to stop littering from cars.

▶ Leaving your junk in a public place is known as fly-tipping. Mattresses, tyres and shopping trolleys are often dumped in the countryside.

450
Some people treat the countryside and other public places as a dumping ground. Big items, such as mattresses, sofas and shopping trolleys, are sometimes dumped on roadsides or in rivers. Besides looking a mess, these things can release poisons as they rot away.

451
The plastic rings that hold cans together can be deadly for wildlife. These stretchy loops are used to hold drinks cans together in packs. As litter, they can get caught around the neck of a wild animal, such as a seagull, and strangle it. Snip the loops open with scissors before throwing them in the bin.

▲ Ducks struggle through a pond polluted with plastic bottles.

▼ Fishing nets left on beaches can endanger wildlife. This one has become tangled around a sea lion's neck.

452
Fishing weights and lines left near rivers and lakes can choke or strangle water wildlife. Weights sometimes contain lead and this can poison water birds, such as swans. People who go fishing should make sure they never leave any of their equipment behind.

197

Reducing waste

453 There are lots of things you can do to reduce waste. When you throw something away, think if it could be recycled or re-used instead. Avoid buying things that will have to be thrown away after one use.

MAKE SOME COMPOST

Make a heap of plant waste, fruit and vegetable skins and grass cuttings in a corner of your garden. It takes a few months to turn into compost. To help it along, mix it around and dig it over with a garden fork. When the compost is ready, you can use it for potting plants or add it to soil in your garden.

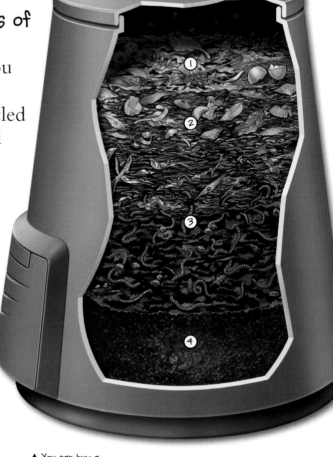

▲ You can buy a specially made compost bin to make compost in, like this one.

454 Instead of throwing away fruit and vegetable peelings, turn them into compost. When your peelings rot down, they turn into a rich, fertile soil that's great for your garden. All you need is a space outside where you can pile up your waste for composting, or you can get a special compost bin.

The composting process

1. Waste, including fruit and vegetable peelings, tea bags, leaves and eggshells, goes in the top.

2. Tiny organisms called microbes start to break down the waste, which makes it heat up.

3. Insects help to break it down even more and worms help air to get into the compost.

4. The compost is brown and moist and should smell earthy.

455 Millions of disposable batteries end up in landfill sites every year. They take a long time to decay and when they do, they release harmful chemicals. Rechargeable batteries can be refilled with energy from the mains and re-used many times.

456 Reduce your waste – pick re-usables, not disposables. Face wipes and disposable nappies, cups and cooking trays are all things that we use once, then throw away. It's greener to use re-useables, such as washable baking trays, cloth tea towels and washable nappies.

457 Lots of the things we buy come wrapped up several times over. We take them home, unwrap them and throw the packaging away. Choose products with less packaging, or none at all.

▼ Much of our rubbish is made up of pointless packaging that we don't really need.

TIME TO DECOMPOSE

Fruit and vegetables	2 days to 6 months
Newspaper	6 months
Drinks cans	100 to 500 years
Disposable nappies	200 to 500 years
Plastic bags	450 years
Plastic bottles	100 to 1000 years +

Cutting pollution

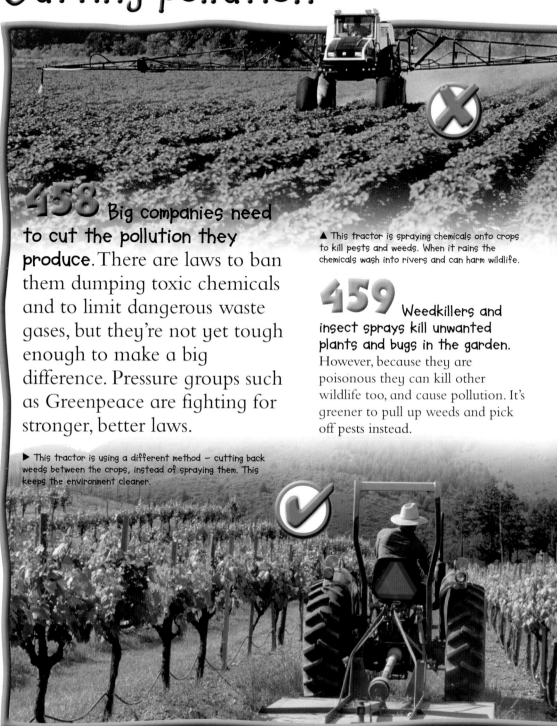

458 Big companies need to cut the pollution they produce. There are laws to ban them dumping toxic chemicals and to limit dangerous waste gases, but they're not yet tough enough to make a big difference. Pressure groups such as Greenpeace are fighting for stronger, better laws.

▲ This tractor is spraying chemicals onto crops to kill pests and weeds. When it rains the chemicals wash into rivers and can harm wildlife.

459 Weedkillers and insect sprays kill unwanted plants and bugs in the garden. However, because they are poisonous they can kill other wildlife too, and cause pollution. It's greener to pull up weeds and pick off pests instead.

▶ This tractor is using a different method – cutting back weeds between the crops, instead of spraying them. This keeps the environment cleaner.

460 Cleaning your house can make the planet dirty!

Strong cleaning chemicals that are washed down the sink can end up in water supplies. Try to use less of them, or use natural, home-made alternatives. A mixture of water and vinegar is great for cleaning windows.

▶ Some companies are now making re-useable washing balls that clean clothes without using any detergent.

461 Paint, paint stripper and varnish contain toxic chemicals.

These chemicals don't break down naturally when they are poured away, which results in pollution. If you can, save them to use again, or see if your local council will collect them for re-using (some councils do this).

462 Shampoo, face creams and make-up are full of polluting chemicals.

Pick greener products that contain natural ingredients. You can even use everyday ingredients, such as olive oil, to make your own skin treatments.

▲ Soap nuts are berries of the soapberry tree. They contain a natural, soapy chemical that can be used to wash clothes.

MAKE A FOOT SOAK

Mix together:
1 tablespoon of fine oatmeal
1 tablespoon of skimmed milk powder
1 teaspoonful of dried rosemary

Spoon the mixture into an old, clean sock and tie a knot at the top. Leave the sock in a bowl of warm water for a few minutes, then soak your feet in the water for 20 minutes.

Wildlife in danger

463 Since humans have existed on Earth, many living things have been destroyed. To make space for cities, farms and roads, people have taken over wild areas, and plants and animals have lost their natural homes, or habitats. This is called habitat loss and it is the main reason why wildlife is in danger.

▲ Wild animals, such as leopards and tigers, are still killed for their fur to make items such as handbags and rugs.

464 Toxic waste, oil spills and pesticides can be deadly for wildlife. In the 1950s, a chemical called DDT was used to kill insects on crops, but it affected other animals including wild birds. It made them lay eggs with very thin shells that cracked easily. The birds began to die out as they could not have chicks.

▼ This bird is covered in oil spilt from an oil tanker (a ship that carries oil). If birds like this aren't cleaned, they will die.

465 Wild plants and animals suffer when we exploit them – use them to meet our needs. Humans hunt wild animals for their skins, meat and other body parts, such as ivory from elephants' tusks. Some people steal wild plants, too. If too many are taken, their numbers fall fast.

◄ These nature reserve wardens in Dzanga–Ndoki National Park in the Central African Republic have caught some poachers hunting protected animals.

QUIZ

What do these words mean?
1. Extinct 2. Species
3. Endangered 4. Habitat

Answers:
1. Died out and no longer existing. 2. A particular type of living thing. 3. In danger of becoming extinct. 4. The surroundings where a plant or animal lives.

466 Human activities have wiped out some species, or types, of living things. When a species no longer exists, it is said to be extinct. The great auk – a large-beaked, black-and-white sea bird – became extinct in the 1850s due to hunting by humans. Many other species are now close to extinction, including the tiger and mountain gorilla.

▼ The orang–utan – a type of ape – is an extremely threatened species, and one of our closest animal cousins.

467 When a creature is in danger of becoming extinct, we call it threatened. Severely threatened species are known as endangered. These labels help to teach people about the dangers to wildlife. They also help us to make laws to try to protect these species from hunters and collectors.

Saving habitats

468 To save wildlife, we need to save habitats. Humans are taking up more and more space and if we don't slow down, there'll be no wild, natural land left. We need to leave plenty of natural areas for wildlife to live in.

▲ These penguins live in Antarctica. Their habitat is ice and freezing water and it could be affected by global warming.

469 One hundred years ago, people went on safari to hunt animals. Today, more tourists go to watch wild animals and plants in their natural habitat – this is called ecotourism and it helps wildlife. Local people can make enough money from tourism, so they don't need to hunt. However, ecotourism can disturb wildlife, so tourists have to take care where they go.

▶ Tourists in a Jeep approach a pride of lions in a nature reserve in South Africa.

470 Nature reserves and national parks are safe homes for wildlife. The land is kept wild and unspoiled to preserve natural habitats. There are also guards or wardens to protect the wildlife and watch out for hunters.

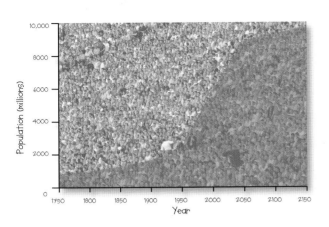

As the human population continues to rise, more and more wild, natural land is being taken over.

471 It can be hard for humans to preserve habitats because we need space too. There are nearly 7 billion (7,000,000,000) humans on Earth today. Experts think this will rise to at least 9 billion. Some countries have laws to limit the number of children people are allowed to have to try to control the population.

▼ A diver explores a coral reef. The corals are home to many species of fish, crabs and shellfish.

472 You can help to keep habitats safe. In the countryside, don't take stones, shells or flowers. Visit nature reserves – your money helps to run them. Don't buy souvenirs made of coral, or other animals or plants, as this encourages hunting and habitat destruction.

I DON'T BELIEVE IT!

The river Thames in London has just 10 percent of the pollution it had in the 1950s because of pollution prevention, and is home to over 100 species of fish.

In the garden

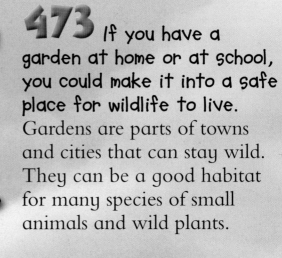

473 If you have a garden at home or at school, you could make it into a safe place for wildlife to live. Gardens are parts of towns and cities that can stay wild. They can be a good habitat for many species of small animals and wild plants.

◀ An insect box provides a home for creatures, such as bees and ladybirds.

474 Wild creatures love a messy garden. If gardens are always tidy there is nowhere for animals to hide. Leave parts of your garden untidy and overgrown – let grass and weeds grow and don't clear up piles of leaves. These areas provide shelter and homes for spiders, beetles, birds and hedgehogs.

▼ Hedgehogs like hiding under leaves. If you have hedgehogs in your garden, don't give them milk as it's bad for them, but try meat scraps, berries and grated cheese instead.

FOOD FOR BIRDS

Here are some snacks to try putting out for garden birds:
Grated hard cheese
Raisins
Sunflower seeds or other seeds
Chopped or crushed nuts
Meat scraps
Fresh, chopped coconut

Avoid putting out dry or salty food, such as stale bread or salted nuts, as it's bad for birds.

475 You can help wild birds by feeding them. Feed birds in winter — there are fewer berries and insects for them to eat at this time of year. Put up a bird table, or hang bird feeders from trees in your garden.

▲ Butterflies such as tortoiseshells like to feed on the flowers of a buddleia bush.

◀ A coal tit and a red squirrel are helping themselves to nuts from this bird feeder.

476 Bees and butterflies feed on nectar — a sweet juice found inside flowers. A garden full of flowers will provide lots of food for insects. They especially like sunflowers, lavender and buddleia bushes.

▶ Sunflowers are great for wildlife. They provide nectar for insects and nutritious seeds for birds.

477 Thick, thorny bushes are brilliant for birds. Some bushes, such as brambles and hawthorns, provide berries that birds like to eat. Thick, tangled bushes also make safe places for birds to build their nests or hide from animals, such as pet cats.

Saving species

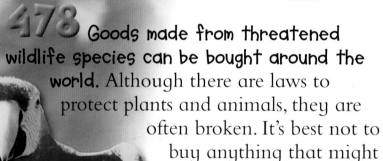

478 Goods made from threatened wildlife species can be bought around the world. Although there are laws to protect plants and animals, they are often broken. It's best not to buy anything that might come from a threatened species, such as ivory, skins, horns or bones.

◄ Parrots are sometimes stolen from the wild as chicks and sold as pets.

480 You or your class could sponsor an endangered animal, such as a tiger. You pay a small fee that goes towards caring for the animal and running the zoo or reserve where it lives. In return, you'll get letters or emails about your animal's progress. Zoos and wildlife organizations can help you to do this.

479 Exotic pets can be exciting, but they are sometimes stolen from the wild. Avoid having an unusual pet such as a rare lizard or parrot. It could be a threatened species that has been taken away from its natural habitat.

◀ A Greenpeace ship (far left) encounters a whaling ship, the Nisshin Maru, in the Antarctic Ocean. Some countries still hunt whales, but campaigning groups such as Greenpeace are trying to stop it.

I DON'T BELIEVE IT!

Millions of sharks, including threatened species, are hunted every year to make shark's fin soup. The soup is an expensive delicacy in China.

481 People still hunt threatened species, even though it's illegal. Many people in the world are very poor and some can't resist hunting a threatened tiger to sell its skin, or a shark to sell its fins. Governments need to try to reduce poverty, to help wildlife as well as people.

482 To help endangered animals, visit your nearest zoo. Most zoos have captive breeding programmes. These help endangered animals to have babies to increase their numbers. Some can then be released back into the wild.

▼ In China, giant pandas are being bred successfully on wildlife reserves. These are just some of the new babies born in recent years.

Forests and farms

483 Every year, over 12 million hectares of forests are logged (cut down). That's an area the size of the country of Malawi in Africa, or the US state of Pennsylvania. Trees do grow again, but we are cutting forests down much faster than they can grow back.

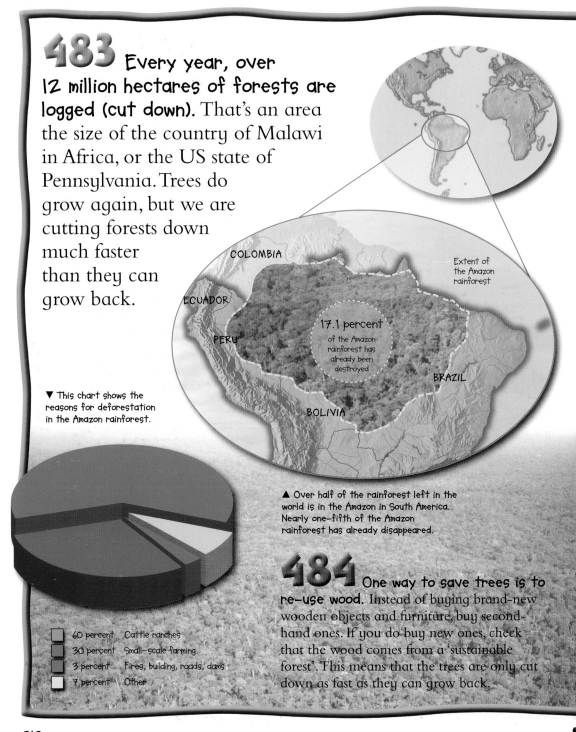

Extent of the Amazon rainforest

COLOMBIA

ECUADOR

PERU

17.1 percent of the Amazon rainforest has already been destroyed

BRAZIL

BOLIVIA

▼ This chart shows the reasons for deforestation in the Amazon rainforest.

- 60 percent — Cattle ranches
- 30 percent — Small-scale farming
- 3 percent — Fires, building, roads, dams
- 7 percent — Other

▲ Over half of the rainforest left in the world is in the Amazon in South America. Nearly one-fifth of the Amazon rainforest has already disappeared.

484 One way to save trees is to re-use wood. Instead of buying brand-new wooden objects and furniture, buy second-hand ones. If you do buy new ones, check that the wood comes from a 'sustainable forest'. This means that the trees are only cut down as fast as they can grow back.

485 Farms take up almost 40 percent of the Earth's land. We need farms to provide us with food – to grow crops and keep animals on – but they have a big impact on the Earth. Most farmland is devoted to one type of crop or animal, so many types of wildlife that live there lose their homes.

▲ Large areas of rainforest in Indonesia and Malaysia have been cut down to make way for oil palm tree plantations. The fruits of the oil palm are harvested for their oil, which can be found in one in ten supermarket products.

486 Organic farming can be a greener way to farm. It doesn't use artificial chemicals, such as pesticides and fertilizers, which means it is good for wildlife and the soil. If you buy organic food and other products, you help to keep the Earth cleaner.

I DON'T BELIEVE IT!

In prehistoric times, forests covered more than half of the Earth's land. Today, almost half of those forests have gone.

487 Buying nuts can help save the rainforests. Some products, such as brazil nuts, grow on rainforest trees. By buying them, you are helping farmers to keep rainforests alive, instead of cutting them down to grow other crops.

▶ As most nuts grow on trees, they are one crop that can be grown without cutting them down.

Seas and coasts

488 Seas and oceans cover the biggest part of the Earth's surface – nearly three-quarters of it! Pollution, global warming and fishing have a huge effect on the sea and its wildlife.

489 Pollution from farms, factories and houses often flows into rivers and ends up in the sea. Tiny sea plants and animals absorb the chemicals. When they are eaten by larger sea creatures, the polluting chemicals are passed on from one animal to the next. Many large sea creatures, such as sharks and polar bears, have been found to have a lot of toxic chemicals in their bodies.

490 Coastal areas are in trouble because of rising sea levels. As the sea rises, tides, tsunamis and storm waves can reach further inland. If the sea rises much more, it could put many coastal cities underwater. The danger of the sea flooding the land is one of the biggest reasons to try to slow global warming down.

◄ In Thailand, signs on beaches and streets give warnings and provide evacuation directions to be used in the event of a tsunami. Thailand is one of the countries that was devastated by the tsunami that struck on December 26, 2004.

491 **For thousands of years, humans have hunted fish.** Today, we are catching so many fish that some types are in danger of disappearing – this is called overfishing. To try to stop it, there are laws to give fishing boats a quota, or limit, on how many fish they can catch.

▼ Low-lying islands, such as this one in Fiji, are in danger of disappearing as sea levels rise.

▶ Cod is one type of fish that has been overfished in some parts of the world.

492 **There's precious treasure in the seabed.** It contains oil – a fossil fuel – and many other useful minerals. However, drilling and digging into the seabed damages wildlife and sea habitats, such as coral reefs. Governments are starting to set up nature reserves in the sea, as well as on land. In these areas, no mining or drilling is allowed.

◀ Oil rigs such as this one are built around a giant drill that bores into the seabed to extract oil.

Water resources

493 **The world is using too much water.**
In many places, water is being pumped out of lakes, rivers and underground wells faster than rain can replace it. As the human population grows, so will the need for water.

▼ Most of the world's freshwater is frozen! The figures below show where the fresh water is found.

Ice caps and glaciers
77.2 percent

Ground water
22.26 percent

Rivers and lakes
0.32 percent

Soil
0.18 percent

Atmosphere
0.04 percent

494 **Global warming is causing huge water problems.**
Some areas are getting more rain and floods, as hotter temperatures lead to more clouds and storms. Floods often pollute water supplies. Other places are becoming hotter and drier, leading to droughts. Either way, global warming is leading to water shortages.

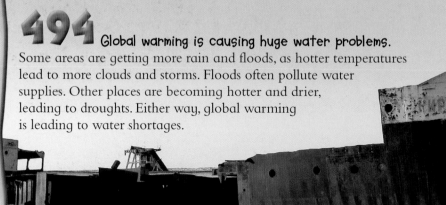

▲ This boat was left high and dry in the Aral Sea in central Asia, which is shrinking because its water has been drained to water crops.

▶ Villagers in Pakistan collect water from a deep well after a rain shower during a drought.

495 In some countries, drinking water comes from the sea.

Seawater is much too salty to drink, but in dry countries, such as Kuwait, they have factories called desalination plants. They take the salt out of seawater to make it fit to drink. However this process uses up lots of energy and is not a long-term solution.

496 Having a green garden saves water! Many

people pave their gardens over for a patio, but rain flows straight off the hard surface and can lead to floods. If gardens are kept as soil and plants, rain soaks into the ground and keeps water supplies topped up.

▼ An aerial view of a desalination plant in Kuwait.

Seawater enters here and is forced through the filter

Salt molecules cannot pass through the filter

Fine filter

Water molecule

▲ The salt is removed from seawater by pushing it through a very fine filter, making it drinkable. This process is called reverse osmosis.

The environment around us

497 The word environment means the place that surrounds us. Planet Earth and all the habitats on it make up our environment. That's why being green is sometimes called environmentalism.

► We need to let as much of the Earth as possible stay in its natural state, such as this beautiful forest in Borneo.

498 As this book shows, the Earth is changing too fast. To be green, and to care for the environment, we need to change the Earth as little as possible. We must reduce the litter, pollution and greenhouse gases that we produce. At the same time we must take less away from it.

TURN YOUR SCHOOL GREEN

One thing you can do to help save the Earth is persuade your school to go green (or greener). Here are some ideas:

• Arrange a recycling rota to collect waste paper from all the classrooms and offices.

• Make posters to put up in the toilets to remind people to save water.

• If there's space, set up a school wildlife garden and compost heap – persuade the kitchen staff to compost food leftovers.

499 Being green is a job for everyone. At home, switching off lights and saving water helps to save the Earth. Towns, communities and businesses can help, too, by arranging recycling collections, or banning plastic bags. Governments are already starting to pass laws to limit things such as pollution, logging and overfishing.

500 Planet Earth is the only home we have. It's also the only home for wild animals and plants. After us, it will be the home of future generations. What we do now will decide whether it ends up a messy, overheated planet, or one that's healthy and safe to live on.

Index

Entries in **bold** refer to main subject entries. Entries in *italics* refer to illustrations.

Index

Index

Acknowledgements

The publishers would like to thank the following sources for the use of their photographs:

Alamy 78 Bryan & Cherry Alexander Photography; 83(t) Bryan & Cherry Alexander Photography; 174(b) BrazilPhotos.com; 182 Tom Uhlman; 200(t) AGStockUSA, Inc.

Corbis 54 Rob Howard; 58 Tom Bean; 74 Wolfgang Kaehler; 75(b) Paul A. Souders; 79(t) Jack Jackson/ Robert Harding World Imagery, (b) Patrick Robert; 81(t) Galen Rowell; 84 Stapleton Collection; 85 Jason Roberts/Push Pictures/Handout/epa; 87 Van Hasselt John/Sygma; 88 Paul Souders; 138(l) Owen Franken; 139 Frans Lanting, (tr) Demetrio Carrasco/JAI; 153(tr) Martin Harvey; 169(br) George Steinmetz; 172 Frans Lanting; 176–177 NASA/Reuters; 181(c) Bettmann; 184(b) Klaus Hackenberg/zefa; 186(t) Jean-Paul Pelissier/Reuters; 187(t) Dean Conger; 190 Arctic-Images; 191(bl) Gideon Mendel; 193 Olivier Maire/eps, (tl) Phil Schermeister; 194–195 Yann Arthus-Bertrand, (bl) Vivianne Moos; 196 Gene Blevins/LA Daily News; 197(b) Ron Sanford; 200(b) Ed Young; 202(t) Mike Segar/Reuters, (b) Desmond Boylan/Reuters; 203(t) Martin Harvey; 207(t) Brian S. Turner/Frank Lane Picture Agency; 209(t) Kate Davidson/epa; 213 Neil Farrin/JAI, (t) Jeffrey L Rotman; 215(t) Reuters, (c) Yann Arthus-Bertrand; 216–217 Frans Lanting

Dreamtime 152(t) Sloth92; 169(tc) Braendan

FLPA 55 Matthias Breiter/Minden Pictures; 56–57 Michio Hoshino/Minden Pictures; 57(br) Patricio Robles Gil/Sierra Madre/Minden Pictures; 62(t) Michio Hoshino/Minden Pictures; 62–63(b) Jim Brandenburg/Minden Pictures; 65 Michio Hoshino/Minden Pictures; 68(t) Michael Quinton/Minden Pictures; 68–69(b) Fritz Polking; 72–73 Norbert Wu/Minden Pictures; 90–91 Colin Monteath/Minden Pictures; 147(tr) Mark Moffett/Minden Pictures; 153(b) Frans Lanting; 154(bl) Jeffrey Oonk/Minden Pictures; 168–169 ImageBroker; 170–171 Cyril Ruoso/JH Editorial/Minden Pictures; 179 Tui De Roy/ Minden Pictures; 201(b) Ulrich Niehoff/Imagebroker; 208–209(b) Katherine Feng/Globio/Minden Pictures

Fotolia.com 138(r) urosr; 140(bl) amaet; 141(r) Impala; 152(b) fivespots; 164(tc) Michael Luckett; 169(tl) Shariff Che'Lah, (tr) Uros Petrovic; 181(b) schaltwerk.de; 198 David Kesti; 204(t) Steve Estvanik; 205(t) Olga Alexandrova; 206(b) Ennoy Engelhardt; 212(b) MiklG; 214 Igor Bekirov

Getty images 134–135 Siegfried Layda; 150–151(t) Roy Toft; 174(tr) Matthias Clamer; 183 China Photos/Stringer; 187(b); 204(b) Per-Anders Pettersson; 211(tl) Dimas Ardian/Stringer

NHPA 80–81(b) Bryan & Cherry Alexander; 82–83 Bryan & Cherry Alexander; 136–137 Nigel J Dennis; 171(tr) Martin Harvey

Photolibrary 59 Sanford/Agliolo; 66 Noel Hendrickson; 70–71 Juniors Bildarchiv; 76 Tim Davis; 140–141 Nick Gibson; 146–147(t) Wave RF; 147(br) Sergio Pitamitz; 157(tr) Mike Powles; 158(l) David M Dennis, (r) Garcia Garcia; 159(br) David Kirkland; 160–161 Wendy Shattil; 162–163 J & C Sohns; 162(bl) Morales Morales; 173(main) Jacques Jangoux; 175 Berndt Fischer

Rex Features 50–51 Lehtikuva Oy; 89(t) Toby Zerna/Newspix; 149 Paul Raffaele

Science Photo Library Cover; 192 Victor Habbick Visions

Still Pictures 75(t) Fred Bruemmer; 91(b) Bruno P. Zehnder

Sunshine Solar Ltd 191(cr)

TopFoto.co.uk 86 ©TopFoto

www.ecozone.co.uk 201(t)

www.firebox.com 189

All other images from the Miles Kelly Archives